Aesthetics: A Very Short Introduction

VERY SHORT INTRODUCTIONS are for anyone wanting a stimulating and accessible way into a new subject. They are written by experts, and have been translated into more than 45 different languages.

The series began in 1995, and now covers a wide variety of topics in every discipline. The VSI library currently contains over 600 volumes—a Very Short Introduction to everything from Psychology and Philosophy of Science to American History and Relativity—and continues to grow in every subject area.

Very Short Introductions available now:

Available soon:

For more information visit our website

www.oup.com/vsi/

Bence Nanay

AESTHETICS

A Very Short Introduction

OXFORD
UNIVERSITY PRESS

Great Clarendon Street, Oxford, OX2 6DP,
United Kingdom

Oxford University Press is a department of the University of Oxford.
It furthers the University's objective of excellence in research, scholarship,
and education by publishing worldwide. Oxford is a registered trade mark of
Oxford University Press in the UK and in certain other countries

Published in the United States of America by Oxford University Press
198 Madison Avenue, New York, NY 10016, United States of America

British Library Cataloguing in Publication Data
Data available

Library of Congress Control Number: 2019946073

ISBN 978-0-19-882661-3

Printed in Great Britain by
Ashford Colour Press Ltd, Gosport, Hampshire

Contents

Acknowledgements

I am grateful for the comments on earlier versions of this book from Nicolas Alzetta, Alma Barner, Felicitas Becker, Constant Bonard, Chiara Brozzo, Denis Buehler, Patrick Butlin, Dan Cavedon-Taylor, Will Davies, Ryan Doran, Peter Fazekas, Gabriele Ferretti, Loraine Gerardin-Laverge, Kris Goffin, Laura Gow, John Holliday, Anna Ichino, Laszlo Koszeghy, Magdalini Koukou, Robbie Kubala, Kevin Lande, Jason Leddington, Hans Maes, Manolo Martinez, Mohan Matthen, Chris McCarroll, Regina-Nina Mion, Thomas Raleigh, Sam Rose, Maarten Steenhagen, Jakub Stejskal, Lu Teng, Gerardo Viera, Allert Van Westen, Dan Williams, Nick Wiltsher and Nick Young and an anonymous referee. Special thanks to Dominic Lopes, who read three different versions of the manuscript. The writing of this book was supported by the ERC Consolidator grant [726251], the FWO Odysseus grant [G.0020.12N] and the FWO research grant [G0C7416N].

List of illustrations

Chapter 1
Lost in the museum

You go to the museum. Stand in line for half an hour. Pay 20 bucks. And then, you're there, looking at the exhibited artworks, but you get nothing out of it. You try hard. You read the labels next to the artworks. Even get the audio guide. Still nothing. What do you do?

Maybe you are just not very much into this specific artist. Or maybe you're not that much into paintings in general. Or art. But on other occasions you did enjoy looking at art. And even looking at paintings by this very artist. Maybe even the very same ones. But today, for some reason, it's not happening.

Sounds familiar? We've all struggled with this. Maybe not in the museum, but in the concert hall, or when we're trying to read a novel before going to sleep. Engagement with art can be immensely rewarding, but it can also go wrong very easily. And the line between the two can be very thin.

I use this example to introduce the topic of aesthetics because what we are trying to have in these situations is a kind of experience that this book is about. And not being able to have it (but trying to do so) really pins down what these experiences are and how important they are for all of us.

While I have used examples from art, this can also happen when we are trying to take in the view from a mountaintop or when we are trying to savour a gourmet meal in vain. Aesthetic engagement (with art, nature, or food) can be a bumpy ride.

Non-elitist aesthetics

Aesthetics is about some special kinds of experiences. Ones we care about a lot. The Greek word '*aesthesis*' means 'perception' and when the German philosopher, Alexander Baumgarten (1714–62) introduced the concept of 'aesthetics' in 1750, what he meant by it was precisely the study of sensory experiences (*scientia cognitionis sensitivae*).

The experiences that aesthetics talks about come on a spectrum. We care about some experiences more than others. Not just the experience of artworks in a museum or of an opera performance. Also the experience of the autumn leaves in the park on our way home from work or even just the light of the setting sun falling on the kitchen table. But aesthetics is also about your experience when you choose the shirt you're going to wear today or when you wonder whether you should put more pepper in the soup. Aesthetics is everywhere. It is one of the most important aspects of our life.

Aesthetics is sometimes considered to be too elitist—by artists, musicians, even by philosophers. This is based on a misunderstanding of the subject, something this book aims to correct. So-called 'high art' has no more claim on aesthetics than sitcoms, tattoos, or punk rock. And the scope of aesthetics is far wider than that of art, high or low. It includes much of what we care about in life.

Witold Gombrowicz (1904–69), the Polish avant-garde novelist, captured this sentiment very elegantly:

The food does not always taste best in first-class restaurants. To me, art almost always speaks more forcefully when it appears in an imperfect, accidental, and fragmentary way, somehow just signaling its presence, allowing one to feel it through the ineptitude of the interpretation. I prefer the Chopin that reaches me in the street from an open window to the Chopin served in great style from the concert stage.

It is not the job of aesthetics to tell you which artworks are good and which ones are bad. Nor is it the job of aesthetics to tell you what experiences are worth having—Chopin in the street or Chopin in the concert hall. If an experience is worth having for you, it thereby becomes a potential subject of aesthetics. You can get your aesthetic kicks where you find them. Aesthetics is not a field guide that tells you which experiences are allowed and which are not. It is not a map that helps you find them either. Aesthetics is a way of analysing what it means to have these experiences. Aesthetics is, and should be, completely non-judgemental.

Here is an evocative example. Fernand Léger (1881–1955), the French painter, describes how he and his friend observed a tailor's shop owner arranging seventeen waistcoats, with corresponding cufflinks and neckties, in the display window. The tailor spent eleven minutes on each waistcoat. He moved it to the left by a couple of millimetres, then went outside, in front of the shop, to take a look. Then went back in, moved it to the right a bit, and so on. He was so absorbed that he didn't even notice that Léger and his friend were watching him. Léger was left somewhat humiliated, pondering how few painters take as much aesthetic interest in their work as this old tailor. And surely even fewer museum-goers. Léger's point, and also the guiding principle of this book, is that the tailor's experience is as worthy of being called aesthetic as any museum-goer's admiring Léger's paintings.

Thinking about aesthetics in this inclusive way opens up new ways of understanding old questions about the social aspect of our aesthetic engagements and the importance of aesthetic values for our own self. It also makes it possible to think about art and aesthetics in a genuinely global manner that does not presuppose the primacy of the 'West'.

Aesthetics or philosophy of art?

Aesthetics is not the same as philosophy of art. Philosophy of art is about art. Aesthetics is about many things—including art. But it is also about our experience of breathtaking landscapes or the pattern of shadows on the wall opposite your office.

This book is about aesthetics. As a result, it is both broader and narrower in scope than a book about philosophy of art would be. Philosophy of art talks about a wide variety of philosophical questions concerning art—metaphysical, linguistic, political, ethical questions. I will not touch most of these questions. There will be no talk of the definition of art for example, of how artworks are different from all the other objects in the world.

Barnett Newman (1905–70), the American abstract painter, famously said that aesthetics is as irrelevant for artists as ornithology is for birds. It should be clear that it is philosophy of art that would be the equivalent of ornithology in this blatant provocation—and not aesthetics. It is philosophy of art that is in the business of categorizing artworks and mulling over differences between different species/genres, not aesthetics. So Newman's quip is really about philosophy of art, not aesthetics. Aesthetics, the study of the very experiences artists are working with and are trying to evoke, is very relevant to each and every artist.

But, of course, artworks can trigger all kinds of experiences and aesthetics does not even talk about all of these. I'm sure an art thief has some kind of experience of the artwork she steals, but this is unlikely to be the kind of experience this book is about. Or imagine that I promise to give you a lot of money if you run through the entire Metropolitan Museum of Art and count how many of the paintings are signed. I'm sure you could do it, but this does not exactly put you in an aesthetic state of mind, however broadly one understands that.

We engage aesthetically with artworks, but we engage with artworks in all kinds of other ways as well. And there are many other things we aesthetically engage with. (Throughout the book I use 'aesthetic experience' and 'aesthetic engagement' more or less interchangeably, acknowledging that aesthetic engagement is something we do and aesthetic experience is what we feel while we are engaging aesthetically.) Art and aesthetics come apart. But this does not mean that we should ignore the connection altogether. Many of our aesthetically valuable moments come from engaging with art.

In other words, art is an important object of aesthetics, but it is by no means privileged. According to an influential strand in 'Western' aesthetics, our aesthetic engagement with art—actually, with high art—is just completely different from our aesthetic engagement with anything else. Not only does this line of thought undersell aesthetics inasmuch as it restricts the importance and relevance of aesthetic moments in our life, but it goes against almost all non-'Western' aesthetic traditions. And this book is a very short introduction to aesthetics. Not a very short introduction to one very specific, albeit historically important, aesthetic tradition—the 'Western' one.

Non-'Western' aesthetics

Artefacts have been made everywhere in the world. Music too. Stories as well. Nonetheless, when you go into almost any major art museum in the world, you are likely to encounter objects made in the 'West' (Europe and, if it's a museum of modern art, maybe also North America—I will use scare-quotes around 'West' throughout the book to indicate that the 'West' is obviously not a unitary concept). If you are looking for objects from other parts of the world, you often need to go to a far-away wing or sometimes even to a different museum. But art is not a 'Western' monopoly, and neither is aesthetics.

People have been theorizing about our experience of art all over the world. Sticking to the European line on aesthetics would be as biased as exhibiting only European artworks in a museum. Islamic, Japanese, Chinese, Indonesian, African, Sumer-Assyrian, Pre-Columbian, Sanskrit, and Balinese aesthetics are all incredibly sophisticated thought systems full of very important observations about experiences of art and other things. No book on aesthetics should ignore them.

In fact, it is 'Western' aesthetics that is, in many ways, the outlier—with its emphasis (or should I say obsession?) on judging, on high art, and on taking aesthetic engagement out of its social contexts. I am not going to pretend to cover all aesthetic traditions in this book. But neither will I focus on uniquely 'Western' ideas that blatantly fail to resonate with the rest of the world, regardless of the prestige of the dead white males who came up with them.

Chapter 2
Sex, drugs, and rock 'n' roll

The experiences that would count as aesthetic in some sense are a diverse bunch. Not just listening to your favourite song or seeing your favourite film. But also watching a 'greatest goals' compilation on YouTube, finally deciding on a pair of shoes, choosing where exactly to put the coffee maker on a kitchen counter. It is quite a challenge to find something these all have in common.

And of course one should not be too inclusive. Philosophers often contrast the experience of art with drug-induced and sexually charged experiences (and also with hedonistic experiences in general, like heavy partying, that the term 'rock 'n' roll' is supposed to capture). So the traditional way of thinking about aesthetics is that we have to somehow draw a line between the aesthetic and the non-aesthetic so that sex and drugs are out, but hairstyle and music are in. How can this be done?

I use this sex, drugs, and rock 'n' roll problem as a backdrop to introducing the most important approaches to aesthetics. I don't actually think that we can maintain a distinction between aesthetic experiences on the one hand and sex, drugs, and rock 'n' roll on the other. All things can be experienced in an aesthetic manner and some drug-induced experiences, for example, could very much count as aesthetic. But going through these approaches to aesthetics helps us to see just how difficult it is to keep the aesthetic and the non-aesthetic apart.

I will talk about four influential accounts of aesthetics, focusing on beauty, pleasure, emotion, and 'valuing for its own sake'. Not just to dismiss them or to show that they are not working. Not to make fun of them either. I'm talking about them because each and every one of them contains some really important pointers to how we should and how we should not think about the domain of aesthetics.

Beauty?

The most widely shared take on aesthetics is that it's about beauty. Just look around in the street—the word 'aesthetics' routinely shows up in beauty salons. And it is tempting to take something like a beauty-salon approach when trying to explain what aesthetics, the philosophical discipline, is about. The general thought is that some things are beautiful, others are not. Aesthetics helps us to keep them apart, and maybe even explain why beautiful things are beautiful.

I call this the 'beauty-salon approach' because in cosmetic surgery or the nail business there are fairly clear conceptions of what is beautiful and what is not. In fact, the main aim is to turn something not-so-beautiful into something more beautiful. And many of those who think that aesthetics is about beauty work with similar assumptions about a division line in the world between those things that are beautiful and those that are not.

The beauty-salon approach solves the sex, drugs, and rock 'n' roll problem with little effort. Aesthetic experiences are experiences of beautiful things. Drug-induced experiences or sexual experiences, or the experience of rock 'n' roll, are not of beautiful things. So they won't count as aesthetic.

It would be too easy to mock this view for its moralizing and judgemental overtones (rock 'n' roll is the devil's music and marijuana is the devil's harvest, and sex is, well, sex), but it is important that the real problem with the beauty-salon approach is not that it draws the division line between the beautiful and the non-beautiful in an elitist or prudish manner. The real problem is that it draws any such division line.

Being beautiful is very different from, say, being red. We can sort all the things in the world into two piles: red things and non-red things. This may not make a lot of sense, but we could do it. But we can't sort all the things in the world into the pile of the beautiful things and the other, non-beautiful pile. At least not if we want beauty to have anything to do with aesthetics. As Oscar Wilde (1854–1900) says, 'no object is so ugly that, under certain conditions of light and shade, or proximity to other things, it will not look beautiful; no object is so beautiful that, under certain conditions, it will not look ugly'.

The point is that beauty is not a feature of objects that remains the same at all times, in all contexts, for all observers. If this concept is to be even remotely useful in aesthetics, it needs to be able to capture the fleeting nature of beauty and the fact that, as Oscar Wilde rightly noted, we sometimes see an object as beautiful and sometimes we don't. This has nothing to do with the debate about whether beauty is in the eye of the beholder—something I will come back to in Chapter 5. Even if beauty is not in the eye of the beholder—even if it is 'objective' in some sense, it is highly sensitive to what context we encounter it in. The beauty-salon approach can't explain this context-sensitivity.

Although the beauty-salon approach has dominated much of the history of 'Western' aesthetics, it is not the only approach when it comes to beauty. Here is an alternative, summarized as this pithy slogan, wrongly (but consistently) attributed to Confucius

(551 BCE–479 BCE): 'Everything has beauty but not everyone sees it.' We don't get two piles then, one for beautiful things and one for non-beautiful things. We only get one pile.

Various streaks of avant-garde also endorsed versions of this view. To return to Léger, he also argues against any kind of 'hierarchies of beauty'. Here is an evocative quote by him:

> Beauty is everywhere: perhaps more in the arrangement of your saucepans on the white walls of your kitchen than in your eighteenth-century living room or in the official museum.

The view then is that anything can appear beautiful and aesthetics is exactly about these beautiful experiences. But what makes an experience aesthetic is not that the thing we experience is beautiful, but that we experience it in a certain way (we experience whatever we experience as beautiful). It's not what we experience but rather the way we experience.

This approach captures the anti-elitist and non-judgemental sentiment that I started out with, but there is a sleight of hand here. This way of connecting beauty and aesthetics in fact makes the concept of beauty superfluous. We can tell this story without talking about beauty at all. Beauty is merely a placeholder for the character of our experience—and not a very helpful placeholder either. If aesthetics is about experiencing things, whatever things, as beautiful, then we would want to know what this means. How do I do that? I'm looking at a painting in the museum and my experience is anything but aesthetic. How do I make it into an aesthetic experience? Experience it as beautiful? This is not very helpful advice.

The beauty-salon approach at least gave us a way of making a distinction between aesthetic experiences and non-aesthetic ones (like, allegedly, experiences of sex, drugs, and rock 'n' roll). Not a very good way, but a way nonetheless. The more democratic approach I connected with Confucius and Léger does not, in itself, tell us much about aesthetic experiences. If we go down this route, we still have a lot of explaining to do about what makes some experiences (but not others) the experiences of something as beautiful. And if we can explain this, then any reference to 'beauty' in all this will merely be a not so helpful label.

Nonetheless, the democratic version of the beauty account has taught us something really important. It's not that some things are aesthetic and some others are not. All things (well, almost all things) can trigger aesthetic engagement. And there is nothing, not even the greatest artwork, that will always do so. The big question is how we can explain this kind of aesthetic engagement and the way it is triggered. You can use the label 'experiencing it as beautiful' as a helpful reminder of what this experience is like. But that is not an explanation of this experience.

We can experience the very same object as beautiful and as not beautiful. The former is an aesthetic experience, the latter is not. And the beauty account owes us an explanation of exactly this difference. This explanation will presumably have to do with the way this experience unfolds, or maybe with the way our attention or emotions are exercised. But it has little to do with beauty.

Pleasure?

Another important concept that is often used when talking about the difference between the aesthetic and the non-aesthetic is pleasure. The general thought is that aesthetics is about pleasure. The non-aesthetic is not. Aesthetic experiences are (often—clearly not always) pleasurable experiences—that's why we like having them. The hope is that we can understand what makes an experience aesthetic if we understand the pleasure it involves.

Not all pleasure is aesthetic. Immanuel Kant (1724–1804) argued at length that what is distinctive of aesthetic pleasure is that it is

11

disinterested. And millions of pages were written about just what this 'disinterested pleasure' might mean. Instead of doing more Kant scholarship, I want to start with the psychology of pleasure.

Psychologists make a distinction between two kinds of pleasure. The first kind of pleasure is what you feel when something unpleasant stops. I will call it 'relief pleasure' because it is triggered by the body's returning to its normal state after a period of perturbation. So if you're ravenously hungry and finally get to eat something, the pleasure you feel is relief pleasure—your body returns to its pre-hunger normal state.

Relief pleasure is short-lived. We're done with the unpleasant things—the pleasure marks the moment of relief. But it's only a moment. And relief pleasure does not motivate. It may be the consequence of something we do, but it does not make us do further things.

Contrast this with what I will call 'sustaining pleasure'. Sustaining pleasure motivates us to keep on doing what we are doing—it sustains our activity. We're walking along the beach and it's very pleasurable. It's not a relief from anything. It just feels good. It can go on for a long time—unlike relief pleasure. And it motivates us to keep on walking.

As the Canadian philosopher Mohan Matthen (1948–), building on these psychological distinctions, points out, one and the same activity can give you relief pleasure in some contexts and sustaining pleasure in another. Eating is a good example. It can give you relief pleasure when you have the first bite after not eating for a day. But it can also give you sustaining pleasure if you are enjoying a gourmet meal.

Aesthetic pleasure is typically sustaining pleasure. You are looking at a painting, and the pleasure you feel motivates you to keep on looking at it. It is an open-ended activity just as walking along the beach is. Our pleasure sustains our continued engagement with the painting. It is sometimes even difficult to tear ourselves away.

This gives us a complicated picture concerning the sex, drugs, and rock 'n' roll problem. Some sexual and drug-induced activities will give us sustaining pleasure. So we can't just reject sex and drugs wholesale and exclude them from the elite circle of aesthetic activities. I think this is an advantage of the account—I don't see why some sexual and drug-induced experiences could not count as aesthetic. And the pleasure account even gives us a pointer about what it is that makes some but not other sexual and drug-induced experiences qualify, namely, sustaining pleasure.

There is a fair amount of psychological research on how sustaining pleasure motivates and helps the ongoing activity. One example is drinking. If you drink a largish amount of a kind of beverage you like, this can lead to sustaining pleasure. You take pleasure in taking a sip, maybe swirling it around your mouth, swallowing, taking another sip, and so on. There is a certain rhythm to it and the pleasure you take in this activity sustains this rhythm, but also fine-tunes it.

We know a lot about the physiological mechanisms involved in this in the case of drinking—how the synchronizing of the working of various muscles leads to the seamless coordination of the processes involved in drinking. But how does it happen in the case of aesthetic engagement? What would be the equivalent of the working of our neck-muscles? No muscles are directly involved in most aesthetic engagement, after all.

Sustaining pleasure motivates and fine-tunes our ongoing aesthetic engagement by means of controlling our attention. No muscles are directly involved in most aesthetic engagement, but attention is very much involved. When you are looking at that painting, the pleasure you take in doing so nudges your attention to keep on engaging. So the account of aesthetic pleasure as

13

sustaining pleasure owes us an account of how our attention is exercised in our aesthetic engagement.

One important reason why we should really clarify what kind of attention is sustained by sustaining pleasure comes from feminist film theory. The British film theorist Laura Mulvey (1941–) argues in her extremely influential essay 'Visual Pleasure and Narrative Cinema' that mainstream films almost always try to trigger 'visual pleasures' that are typically the male visual pleasures of voyeurism. The main protagonist the audience is encouraged to identify with tends to be male and we are often encouraged to see the women who show up in these films through the eyes of this male protagonist. This highly sexualized 'male gaze' as Mulvey calls it is what constitutes the visual pleasure of narrative cinema.

This 'visual pleasure' is sustaining pleasure by any account (it encourages us to keep on looking), but it is clearly very different from the kind of disinterested aesthetic pleasure aesthetics talks about. So the pleasure account really needs to say more in order to keep aesthetic and non-aesthetic pleasures apart. And, again, a big part of this explanation will have to do with the mental activity that the pleasure maintains, which will have a lot to do with what we are attending to (and how we do so).

Emotions?

The third approach to delineating the aesthetic domain focuses on emotions. The general thought is that aesthetic experiences are emotional experiences. So understanding what makes aesthetic experiences different from other kinds of experiences would be to understand what kind of emotion is triggered here.

Iris Murdoch (1919–99), the Irish novelist, took literature (and art in general) to be 'a sort of disciplined technique for arousing certain emotions'. And George Kubler (1912–96), one of the most influential art historians of the last century, said that one simple way of thinking about art would be as 'an object made for emotional experience'. As a sociological assessment about art, this may have sounded more convincing in 1959, when Kubler wrote it, than in 2019. After all, much of contemporary art tries to stay as far away from our emotions as possible, preferring a merely intellectual or sometimes a merely perceptual engagement (as in the case of conceptual art and op art). But if we take Murdoch's and Kubler's claims to be about aesthetic engagement and not about art, then it amounts to taking aesthetic experiences to be emotional experiences.

The question is: what kinds of emotions are involved? Always the same kind of emotion in all aesthetic engagement? Or different emotions, depending on what we are engaging with and how we do so?

The more extreme view is that it is always the same emotion that we have in all cases of aesthetic engagement. If we have that emotion, it is an aesthetic engagement, if we don't it's not. But what would this 'aesthetic emotion' be? There is no shortage of candidates, from wonder and being moved to the contemplation of formal features. But it is easy to come up with examples of aesthetic engagement where none of these emotions are present.

One striking feature of aesthetic engagements is their diversity: our aesthetic experience of the Grand Canyon and of a Billie Holiday song would involve very different emotions. Looking for just one catch-all emotion that we would have in all these cases would amount to ignoring or papering over the diversity of aesthetics.

And even the same object can trigger very different emotions in different circumstances. One of the weirdest stories I have heard about art was from a very good friend of mine who went to the San Francisco Museum of Modern Art after every first date and sat down in front of a very big Mark Rothko painting to figure out

15

how she felt about the new potential romantic partner. It was not just an environment to think about someone, it was her reaction to the painting that was coloured by the previous encounter. The emotions this large abstract painting evoked on these occasions, I was told, were very different. If aesthetic experience of one painting can lead to such diverse emotions, how could all aesthetic engagement be brought under the umbrella of just one kind of special 'aesthetic emotion'?

Nonetheless, it is undeniable that aesthetic engagement can be, and often is, an emotional affair. Art can make you cry. And nature too. The link between aesthetics and emotions is something all aesthetic traditions, from Islamic and Sanskrit to Japanese and Chinese aesthetics, talk about.

Any account of aesthetic experiences would need to take emotions seriously. But this does not mean that emotions are the make-or-break conditions for having an aesthetic experience. Is only aesthetic engagement emotional? Clearly not. Sex, drugs, and rock 'n' roll can be very emotional—maybe even more so than some of the aesthetic examples I have been using. And it could be argued that almost everything we do is emotion-infused in some sense. So the emphasis on emotions will not be too helpful when looking for what is special about the aesthetic.

Conversely, is aesthetic engagement always emotional? When Fernando Pessoa (1888–1935), the Portuguese poet and writer, describes his aesthetic experience as 'drifting without thoughts or emotions, attending only to my senses', this sounds like a familiar form of aesthetic engagement where emotions take the back seat. In at least some cases of aesthetic experience, it is the sensory that dominates, not the emotional.

Even the contemplation of formal features, one of the alleged examples for 'aesthetic emotions', could be thought to be a perceptual and not an emotional affair. Susan Sontag (1933–2004), the American art critic, for example, characterizes aesthetic experience as 'detached, restful, contemplative, emotionally free, beyond indignation and approval'.

Emotion may not be what makes aesthetic experiences aesthetic. But the emotion accounts of aesthetics are still important inasmuch as they highlight just how emotions can be a crucial part of aesthetic experiences. Any account of aesthetics needs to tell a story about how emotional and aesthetic experiences can be, and often are, intertwined.

For its own sake?

Susan Sontag talks about aesthetic experience as detached. Detached not just from emotions, but from indignation, approval, and also practical considerations. And this is the last popular candidate for keeping the aesthetic and the non-aesthetic apart: aesthetic engagement is engagement for its own sake. We don't do it in order to achieve some other, further goal. We do it just for the aesthetic kicks.

This proposal comes in many flavours. Some talk about valuing for its own sake: when we have an aesthetic experience, we value what we are experiencing (or maybe the experience itself) for its own sake. I will not say much about this line of reasoning, because I am not even sure that we are valuing anything when we have aesthetic experiences, let alone valuing things for their own sake. In any case, that would depend on one's account of value and I am definitely not opening that can of worms here. What do I value when I gaze at the specks of dust dancing in a beam of sunshine? The specks of dust? Or am I valuing my own experience? What does it even mean to value one's own experience? That I like to have it? Giving it a thumbs up? If we can formulate the 'for its own sake' account without relying on the concept of valuing, we really should try to do so.

But we can avoid talking about values and focus on just why we are doing what we are doing when engaging aesthetically. Are we trying to achieve something else or are we doing it only for its own sake? If I read a novel so that I can pass a test in my literature class, I do one thing (read the novel) in order to achieve something else (pass the test). If I read it for just reading it, that's closer to the aesthetic domain. But the aesthetic experience can kick in even though I started reading it because of the literature class. In that case, I am not doing it *purely* for its own sake, but I am nonetheless engaging with it aesthetically. And that doesn't mean that my engagement is necessarily less aesthetic. These intermediate cases show that 'doing it for its own sake' is not the holy grail of aesthetics.

Here is another way to capture the 'for its own sake' intuition. Some activities only make sense if they reach an end point or a goal. They are done in order to achieve something. They should be completed. You can't do them just a little bit. Like running a marathon in under four hours.

With activities of this kind, there are two options. You either achieve the goal or you don't. If you don't, then your frustrated desires lead to even stronger desires that are also likely to be frustrated. If you do, well, then four hours is for losers and 3.45 is the new goal. Then 3.30. And so on. There is always a higher mountain to climb.

Luckily not all activities are like this. Some other activities you can do just a little bit. They make sense even if you don't complete them. They are not done to achieve a goal. Like running for the sake of running.

Some things you do for the trophy; some things for the process itself. We need both. Very few people have jobs where we can just enjoy the process of whatever we are doing without any pressure to achieve anything. There are always goals, deadlines, promotion criteria.

And even in our free time much of what we do is geared towards some very specific goal. We cook a meal with the ultimate purpose to serve it to our friends, not just cook aimlessly. So we can't avoid activities we do for the achievement. But we need a healthy balance between activities we do for achievements and activities we do for the process itself.

Aesthetic engagement is not a trophy activity. It is, if it goes well, a process activity. You don't do it for the trophy. It makes sense to do it even though you don't follow it through to its goal or end point, because it has no goal or end point. You can look at a painting for just a little bit. This activity has no natural (or unnatural) end point. Aesthetic engagement is an open-ended activity.

Any account of aesthetic engagement needs to explain this important feature: that it is open-ended and a process, not a trophy activity. But this won't be the cut-off mark that divides the aesthetic from the non-aesthetic either. I have been focusing on examples like looking at a painting, where there really is no end point to the activity. But in other examples of aesthetic engagements, there is an end point. Sonatas and films have a very natural end point, namely, when they are over. We can think about them after they are over, but in some very important sense, there is an end point to the experience itself. These aesthetic activities are very much unlike the timeless contemplation of paintings in this respect.

So while the process activity is an important aspect of some cases of aesthetic engagement, it is not a universal feature of all aesthetic engagement. We could make a distinction *within* the category of aesthetic engagements—some of them are goal-directed, some others are not. But the lack of goal-directedness is not what defines this category.

Where does this leave us with the sex, drugs, and rock 'n' roll issue? As in the case of the pleasure-centred account, the emphasis on doing things for their own sake also divides up the category of sexual and drug-induced experiences. Aldous Huxley (1894–1963) wrote an entire book about how his own drug-induced experiences were detached in exactly the way aesthetic experiences are detached. Again, I take this to be the right approach to sex and drugs—some of these should be part of the domain of aesthetics. Nonetheless, the four standard approaches to aesthetics still failed to give us a clear account of where exactly this domain starts and where it ends.

The 'for its own sake' account clearly captures an important aspect of aesthetic experiences, but this is not the only important aspect. Whatever the final account of the distinction between aesthetic and non-aesthetic will be, it needs to capture the importance of doing things in an open-ended way for their own sake.

Attention?

What we have learned from accounts of beauty is that if we set the beauty-salon approach aside, aesthetics is often about experiencing things as beautiful, where 'as beautiful' is a placeholder for some character of our experiences, which needs to be filled in by any account of aesthetics. Emotion-centred accounts highlight the importance of emotions in our experience, but it still needs to be worked out just how aesthetic experiences are coloured by emotions.

The pleasure-based accounts emphasized the importance of sustaining pleasure, but they are incomplete if they fail to specify what form of attention is involved in such sustaining pleasure. And the 'for its own sake' accounts, as long as we ditch the concept of valuing, push the importance of open-ended, detached, process activities.

I will argue that these accounts all point in the same direction, namely, that what is special about aesthetics is the way we exercise our attention in aesthetic experiences. This can help us explain how experiencing something as beautiful qualifies as aesthetic and also what makes these experiences emotionally infused. Attention was the missing piece in the pleasure-based accounts and talking about the detached open-ended exercise of attention captures much of the 'for its own sake' accounts. As Marcel Proust (1871–1922) said, 'Attention can take various forms and the job of the artist is to evoke the most superior of these.'

Chapter 3
Experience and attention

What all things aesthetic have in common is something very simple: the way you're exercising your attention. This can also happen if this experience is drug-induced or sexually charged (or both). And it often does not happen even when you are staring at a masterpiece.

The difference attention makes

Remember *Goldfinger*? It was one of the better James Bond films (made in 1964). This is the one where the gold-obsessed villain, Auric Goldfinger, schemes to blow up the entire federal gold reserve in Fort Knox. Here he is (Figure 1).

It's an old film, but if you've seen it recently, say, in the last couple of years, it's impossible not to notice the uncanny resemblance between the look of the villain Goldfinger and, well, the 45th president of the US (Figure 2).

Once you've seen this similarity, it's very difficult to unsee it. And it really messes with your mind when you watch the movie, especially given that Goldfinger blows up the federal gold reserve in order to increase the value of his own gold holdings. For me, at least, this now takes a lot away from the enjoyment of the film.

1. Auric Goldfinger, the main villain of the James Bond movie
Goldfinger (1964).

2. Donald J. Trump, the 45th president of the United States
of America.

Attending to the similarity between Goldfinger and Donald J. Trump can make a huge difference. It can change your experience in an aesthetically significant way. This highlights the importance of which features of the artwork we pay attention to. Paying attention to an irrelevant feature could and would derail our experience.

In this example, the aesthetic difference this shift of attention triggers is likely to be a negative one. But it doesn't have to be.

Attending to a relevant feature can completely transform your experience, as in the case of a 16th-century Flemish landscape painting by Bruegel (Figure 3). It's half landscape, half seascape, a nice diagonal composition, with the peasant at the centre ploughing a field with great concentration. A quaint everyday scene; nothing very dramatic. Until you read the title: *The Fall of Icarus*.

What? Where is Icarus? I don't see anyone falling. What does this peasant have to do with that dramatic mythological event? You scan the picture for some trace of Icarus and then you find him (or at least his legs, as he's just fallen into the water) just below the large ship tucked away in the bottom right corner.

My guess is that your experience is now very different. While the part of the canvas where Icarus's legs are depicted was not a particularly salient feature of your experience of the painting before (perhaps you didn't even glance at it), now everything else in the picture seems to be somehow connected to it.

Maybe you experienced the picture as disorganized before, but attending to Icarus's legs pulls the picture together. (This, in any case, seems to be the effect Bruegel was aiming for almost 500 years ago.)

Here is another example, this time involving music. In music it can make a huge difference whether you're attending to the bass

3. Pieter Bruegel the Elder, *The Fall of Icarus* (c.1555), Royal Museums of Fine Art, Brussels.

or the melody. But there are cases where this difference is even more salient. The first canon in Johann Sebastian Bach's *A Musical Offering* (1747) is a fugue-like piece for two instruments. But there is a twist: the two instruments play the very same melody—one from beginning to end, the other backwards, starting at the end and moving backwards.

This is difficult to spot without seeing the music sheet. However, once you have noticed it, it's impossible not to pay attention to this feature of the music. And this is exactly why Bach wrote this piece—to show off the extent of his skill. Attending to this feature is likely to make a positive aesthetic difference.

Here's a somewhat less elitist example from the sitcom *How I Met Your Mother* (CBS, 2005–14). Much of the nine seasons and more than 200 episodes of this sitcom was about the complicated romance and wedding of the dream-couple Barney and Robin. The last season was dedicated in its entirety to their wedding. But then (spoiler alert!) came the very last episode and the very last two minutes of the finale, where the showrunners decided to break up the dream-couple and get Robin back together with Ted.

The fans were outraged. This finale was voted the worst moment of television that year. This twist at the very end made many hardcore *How I Met Your Mother* fans burn all their merchandise and memorabilia, but it also achieved something else. If you manage to get yourself to watch the entire nine seasons again, it is difficult not to see the unfolding story very differently. Moments between Ted and Robin will grab your attention much more easily. And you attend to the dynamics between the three characters very differently from the way you did when you had no idea that this would be the ending.

This trick has been widely used in feature films. One way of getting the audience to spend even more money on a film is to get them to watch it again. And films of certain aspirations do this by revealing something at the very end that changes everything, so much so that, seeing the film for the second time, knowing what you know now, will be a very different experience. Christopher Nolan's *Memento* (2000) and *Inception* (2010) are famous examples, but there are many others. You have very little idea what's going on until the end. And when you see these films for the second time, you see them very differently, because you attend to very different features of the story.

Here is another example, this time not involving art. It is about the worst meal I've ever had. My wife was about to give birth to our first child. I drove her to the hospital in a hurry and then had to go back to pick up all the many things necessary for the hospital stay. I was starving, but I obviously wanted to rush back as soon as I could. So I stuck some leftover Chinese food into the microwave while I was packing the bag. Then the food was way too hot, but I had no time to let it cool down, so I forced it down, burning my mouth quite badly. Not a great culinary experience. But I was out of the house in three minutes!

I said it was 'some leftover Chinese food', but in fact it was the doggy bag from the best Chinese restaurant in town, where we had dinner the night before—really excellent food. I wouldn't say it was the best meal I've ever had, but it was a pretty good meal. Not so much the day after. But then what was the difference? The obvious answer is that it was a difference in attention. There were lots of things I was attending to while feverishly stuffing diapers and swaddling clothes into a suitcase, but the food was not among them.

What you are attending to makes a huge difference to your experience in general. And it also makes a huge difference to your experience of artworks. It can completely ruin your experience, as will happen when you watch *Goldfinger* next time (sorry about that!). Or it can make your experience even more rewarding. And in some cases, it can directly confront you with how differently the same artwork appears to you depending on what you're attending to.

27

But then the question of attention becomes extremely important for anyone interested in aesthetics. Not just for academic philosophers and art historians—for everyone. Imagine that you are sitting in a museum, trying to make sense of the artwork in front of you. What is it that you're supposed to pay attention to? The artwork in front of you has lots of features; it was made by an artist who, no doubt, had a lot of things to say about it. Are you supposed to pay attention to those features of the artwork that the artist found important? Or are you just supposed to pay attention to what the audio guide tells you to?

When we engage with an artwork, we invariably ignore some of its features and focus our attention on others. We ignore the cracks in the paint and focus our attention on other features of the painting's surface; we abstract away from the cracks. When looking at a Romanesque church that was rebuilt in the Baroque era, we may try to ignore the Baroque elements in order to admire the medieval structure. Again, we are attempting to abstract away from some features of the artwork.

But how do we know what features of an artwork we should be paying attention to and what features we should ignore or actively abstract away from? There are no easy answers or cheap shortcuts, I'm afraid. Attention can make or break your aesthetic enjoyment. It can be dangerous—see the *Goldfinger* case—but it can also be, if allocated in the right way, very rewarding aesthetically. We should do more to try to understand what we attend to, and how we do so in aesthetic engagement.

The focus of attention

We know a lot about attention from perceptual psychology and we also know the huge difference it can make to our experience. One of the most celebrated recent experiments about attention demonstrates this nicely. You are shown a short clip of people playing basketball: a team dressed in white against a team

28

dressed in black. Your task is to count how many times the former team passes the ball around. While doing this, more than half of the experimental subjects fail to notice that a man in a gorilla costume walks in the frame, makes funny gestures, spends seven full seconds there, and then leaves. If you're not trying to do any counting tasks, you immediately spot the gorilla. So what you're attending to has serious consequences for whether you spot a man in a gorilla costume bang in the middle of the screen. This phenomenon has a fancy name: 'inattentional blindness'.

Here is a funny and rarely mentioned thing about this experiment: it does not work if you count the number of times the other team—the team dressed in black—passes the ball around. The reason for this is that, well, the gorilla costume is black. If you're attending to the team in white, everything else is noise—the other team, the gym, the gorilla costume. You ignore it; you screen it out.

But when you are attending to the team in black, you will notice the gorilla costume, because it is also black. This should not come as a surprise. When you are trying to flag down a cab, you are seeing every car as either yellow or not yellow (or whatever colour cabs are in your city). The cars that are not yellow are as if they were not there at all. They are noise, to be screened out. Also, when you're looking for Waldo in the *Where is Waldo* books, whatever is not red and white striped is just there to throw you off: you should just ignore it.

Much of our time is spent on attending to some very specific features of what we see and ignoring the rest. When we're trying to do some demanding task, for example, solving the crossword puzzle quickly, there is so much we are trying to ignore so that it does not distract us: anything we smell, hear, and much of what's in our visual field (besides the crossword puzzle). We are natural born ignorers.

And where would we be without this amazing capacity to just shut out much of the world around us? Our mind has limited capacity: if we want to concentrate on something, we need to ignore everything else. And most of the time we do need to concentrate on something: our breakfast, the drive to work, the work itself, and so on.

We understand the psychological mechanisms of how we do this fairly well. Even the earliest stages of our visual processing are highly selective: it only processes information that is relevant in that moment. Everything else is discarded. Some features of the gorilla are discarded as irrelevant for the task at hand as the task only involves attending to what the team in white does and that turns anything black (including the gorilla) into background features.

Your experience depends on what you are attending to. If you shift your attention, your experience will also change. Your experience of the very same concert hall will be very different, depending on whether you are looking for an empty seat or your friend in the crowd. In the former case, all people will melt into the background and the empty seats will pop out. In the latter case, those faces will pop out that are similar to your friend's. Very different experiences indeed.

But how does attention characterize our aesthetic experiences? Here we need to talk not just about *what* we attend to but also about *how* we do so. There are different ways of attending and some of these are more conducive to having (at least some kinds of) aesthetic experiences than others.

Ways of attending

One of the important lessons of the inattentional blindness studies is that whatever we are not attending to just fails to show up in our experience. It is as if we were blind to it. When we did not attend to the gorilla, we did not see the gorilla—we had a fully gorilla-free experience. So not attending to anything entails not having any experience whatsoever.

If you have an amazing meal in a gourmet restaurant, but it is on the occasion of an important business lunch where you really need to impress your boss, you are very unlikely to enjoy the meal. As far as culinary pleasures are concerned, it might as well have been mediocre diner food. Your attention is directed elsewhere, not at the food. Attention is a limited resource: something's gotta give.

One basic distinction vision scientists and psychologists make about attention is that it can be focused or distributed. When you follow the trajectory of five different dots on the screen simultaneously, your attention is distributed. If you are following just one, your attention is focused. These are absolutely routine concepts in psychology when it comes to describing and understanding so-called 'visual search' tasks (tasks like looking for Waldo).

This is a distinction about how many objects we are attending to. But every object has many different features. My coffee cup has colour, shape, weight, and so on. We can attend to one and the same object, but to different features of this object. Attending to the colour of the cup or attending to its weight would give rise to very different experiences. If you shift your attention from the weight of the cup to the colour of the cup, your experience changes. So in the same way that we have a choice about whether we attend to one object or five objects, we also have a choice about whether we attend to one feature of an object or five such features.

So we get not two but four different ways of attending:

(i)   One object, one feature,
(ii) Many objects, one feature,
(iii) Many objects, many features, and
(iv) One object, many features.

This would be nice and logical, but (iii) is not actually an option—this is just not the way our visual system is built. Distributing our attention across five different objects at the same time is tough. In fact, we can only do it for less than a minute even in the most ideal circumstances. After that, we are completely exhausted mentally. And five objects is our absolute limit: we can't do any of this if it is not five, but six different objects. So distributing attention across objects puts a serious strain on the resources, even if it is only one feature we are after. It just doesn't work if we are trying to attend to many features of many objects. We end up losing either some objects or some features from the centre of our attention.

But the other three ways of attending are all very familiar. Take all the objects that are on your kitchen counter. You can pick out one of them, say, a coffee cup, and attend to its colour. This is attending to one and only one feature of one and only one object. You can attend to those objects that happen to be red. That's attending to one and only one feature of many objects. And you can attend to the coffee cup but without zooming in on any particular features.

Attending to one feature of one object happens a lot—each time we are performing some precision task: peeling an apple, for example: only one feature of the apple is interesting here and we will ignore all else (for example, its colour). Attending to one feature of many objects happens even more often: every time we are looking for something, for example.

When I'm looking for a cab, this is exactly what I'm doing. I am looking for exactly one feature of all these cars: whether they are yellow. Running through the airport to catch my flight also involves this way of attending. There are many objects of my attention: all the people and suitcases in my way. But only one feature of these matters to me, namely, how I can get around them. All other features are irrelevant and they are ignored.

I am not attending, for example, to how many of the passengers had a moustache.

What is a bit less common is attending to multiple features of one and the same object. When you are trying to enjoy your very expensive meal in the gourmet restaurant or admiring a painting, you are attending to one thing: the food you're eating and the artwork. But the question is about what features of the food or the painting you are attending to.

So the choice is simple: you can be completely obsessed and preoccupied with one and only one feature of what you see. And sometimes this is what is needed when performing some difficult task. But you can also attend to many features of the very same object. And this is where things get interesting.

Attending to many features of the same object does not guarantee aesthetic experiences. But it is a good starting point. When James Bond is feverishly trying to dismantle a ticking bomb, without having any idea which part is doing what, he is attending to many features of one object. But I doubt that this would be an experience he would want to repeat.

What is also needed is that our attention to the many features of the same object is free and open-ended. What James Bond does is this: he hectically moves around his super-focused attention from one part of the bomb to another, in search of a way to make it stop. He knows exactly what he needs to do, just doesn't know how to do it. He is attending to many features but his attention to all of these features is razor-sharp.

When we have certain kinds of aesthetic experiences, we are doing the exact opposite of this: we are not looking for anything in particular. We are attending to multiple features of the not very unusual scene in front of us, but we are not trying to focus either on any feature in particular or on any group of features. Our attention is free and open-ended.

I have made many distinctions, but there is only one that matters for us now. The distinction between open-ended and not open-ended (or, as I will call it, 'fixated') attention. All open-ended attention is distributed, but not all distributed attention is open-ended—for example, James Bond's isn't. Distributed attention is a good start if we want to have open-ended attention, but it is not enough.

When peeling an apple, our attention is fixated (maybe not the attention of professional apple-peelers, but definitely mine). It is fixated on one feature of one object. This is fixated and focused attention. Our attention is also fixated when we are looking for a cab, only zooming in on one feature of all the cars: the yellow colour. But Bond's attention is also fixated, this time fixated on many features of the bomb. This is fixated and distributed attention. None of these experiences involve open-ended attention and none of them are much fun.

The original distinction from vision science was between focused and distributed attention. But distributed attention is not a guarantee of open-endedness. When you look for a cab, your attention is distributed (across objects), but not open-ended at all. And James Bond's attention is also distributed (across properties), but not open-ended. I reserve the label of 'open-ended attention' to those ways of attending when we distribute our attention among many features of an object, but not with a specific aim or goal in mind.

Fixated attention is exhausting in the long run. Open-ended attention is a form of relaxation for the mind or at least the perceptual system. And our perceptual system really likes a bit of relaxation now and then.

Here is an analogy that may be helpful: working out. You can exercise only your biceps. Obsessively, over and over again. This would be the equivalent of focusing your attention on one feature only. But you can also exercise several muscles at the same time—say, exercising your biceps while being on the treadmill. This would correspond to attending to many features of the same object. But there is nothing open-ended about either of these.

Exercise is good for you, of course, but exercising all day every day is just too much. You also need to relax. And relaxation does not mean being motionless, but, say, leisurely strolling down the street, moving many of your muscles, but none of them too much. Now this would be the equivalent of open-ended attention.

One big difference is this: very few of us exercise all day long. But we do attend in a focused manner most of the time. Otherwise there would be a lot of dropped plates, spilled milk, and traffic accidents. So we need to be extra careful what we do when we do not absolutely have to attend in a focused manner, because these precious moments are rare.

And just as your body needs some downtime when you're not exercising any of your muscles, your perceptual system also needs some downtime, when your attention is not fixated. It would be just plain silly to start exercising a different muscle as soon as you're out of the gym. And it is plain silly to spend those rare moments when we do not need to be fixated on avoiding traffic jams or on trying not to mess up our promotion with more fixated attention. Open-ended attention is the mind's downtime and without it life would be tough.

I'm not saying that aesthetic experience is all about relaxing the perceptual system. But if the perceptual system is overstretched, the aesthetic experience is unlikely to happen. Open-ended attention is special. It allows us to compare two seemingly unrelated shapes in a painting. To trace the way the violin's melody provides a counterpoint to the piano's. Or to attend to the contrasts or parallels between the meal's ingredients. This way of attending is what is special about at least some kinds of aesthetic experiences.

But not all of them. While some aesthetic experiences seem to be open-ended experiences, you may not recognize some of your strongest aesthetic experiences in this characterization at all. Some of your strong aesthetic experiences might involve fixated and even focused attention. Not detachment but strong attachment to what you see. As the French avant-garde film-maker, Danièle Huillet (1936–2006), said: 'We want people to lose themselves in our films. All this talk about "distanciation" is bullsh*t.' I will come to these. But at least some typical aesthetic experiences involve open-ended attention.

The freedom of perception

Attention in many aesthetic contexts is free and open-ended. James Bond's quest to defuse the bomb was neither. He was blatantly not free to attend to any features of the bomb—it would have been stupid to attend to the colour harmony among the wires he was contemplating cutting, for example. And it was very clearly not an open-ended process.

This connection between open-ended attention and freedom is more than a metaphor. When our attention is open-ended, we are not looking for anything specific. We are happy to find what we find, but there is no specific quest to complete. This does not mean that we're not interested. But we just don't have anything specific that we are looking for. Attending in this open-ended manner liberates our perception.

When we are looking at a painting we have never seen before, we often move around our attention among the many features of the work: look here, look there. But we have no clear idea what it is that we're after. If this is a search, it is a search without constraints, without no-go areas. Anything (or almost anything) can be potentially interesting and relevant.

We are incredibly good at ignoring and discounting almost everything we see, so that we can attend to what is important. But when our attention is open-ended, we let ourselves be surprised. It is a much less predictable state than fixated attention and it is this lack of predictability that makes it much more rewarding.

Attending is an action—it is an action we are performing all the time we are awake. And like all other actions, we sometimes perform it freely and sometimes not so freely. Most of the time, not so freely. Most of the time, attention has no-go areas. In fact, the vast majority of areas are no-go areas when our attention is fixated. What we are not fixated on is a mere distraction—it is off limits.

But when our attention is open-ended, it can roam freely. And this freedom also explains many important characteristics of the way attention works in aesthetic contexts. For example, the sad truth is that you can't just count to three and make your attention open-ended at will. In order to try to soften the focus of your attention, making it more open-ended, this act of trying is itself an exercise in fixated attention, which goes against anything open-ended. Trying not to try is not easy to pull off.

Also, open-ended attention needs time. If you're hurried, it's not likely to happen. It's easy to see why. The open-endedness of attention is jeopardized when we are in a rush. We can't let our attention roam freely, because we need to wrap things up in thirty seconds.

Think of attention like butter. It is a limited resource but it can be applied in different ways. It can be spread thinly or thickly. If it is spread across a number of potentially interesting features, it is spread so thinly that each such feature gets less. The attention these features get is softer, milder, less piercing. It is so much more enjoyable.

Aesthetic attention

Open-ended attention is an important feature of aesthetic experiences. Is it a make-or-break condition? Very unlikely. It captures what has been a very influential form of aesthetic experience in a very specific time period (roughly, in the last couple of hundred years) in a very specific part of the world (roughly, the 'West'). We have very little evidence about whether people in medieval times went in for open-ended attention and, more crucially, it might be on its way out in our current smartphone-obsessed times, which are not exactly conducive to open-ended attention. As Marina Abramović (1946–), the avant-garde performance artist, said, 'Today, our attention is less than the television advertisement. We're looking at six or seven problems constantly.' That doesn't exactly sound open-ended.

People like Fernando Pessoa, Susan Sontag, or Marcel Proust wrote beautifully about aesthetic experiences where attention is open-ended and it is important to understand what kind of experiences they were talking about. But these are not the only kind of experiences that would count as aesthetic. Nonetheless, taking the role of attention seriously can help us to say something about less open-ended aesthetic experiences as well.

When we have an aesthetic experience, we don't just attend to the object we see. We also attend to the quality of our experience. Importantly, we attend to the relation between the two. Most of the time, we are attending to the objects around us, without any attention to our experience of them. In a traffic jam, I tend to attend to the car in front of me, the traffic light turning red, the pedestrians in my way.

However, we can also attend to how seeing a certain object hits us. This would mean attending to the relation between an object and the quality of our experience of this object. This does not mean that we direct our eyes inward and are completely absorbed by our own experience only. It is important that both the object and the quality of our experience of this object are part of what our attention latches onto.

To use a very prosaic example, when we are looking at an apple, we can attend to the features of the apple. Or we can attend to the features of our experience of the apple. Or we can attend to both, and the relation between the two. Attending this third way is what I take to be a crucial (and maybe even close to universal) feature of aesthetic experience.

Here is an appeal to authority. Fernando Pessoa describes aesthetic experience in very similar terms. As he says, 'true experience consists in reducing one's contact with reality whilst at the same time intensifying one's analysis of that contact'. Intensifying one's analysis of the contact to the experienced object is exactly what I mean by attending to the relation between the experienced object and the quality of our experience.

There are many ways of attending to the relation between the experienced object and the quality of our experience. In much of this chapter I talked about one specific way of achieving this by means of open-ended attention, but it is not the only way. One consequence of open-ended and unrestricted attention is that our attention can roam freely; not just on features of the perceived object, but also on features of our experience.

Choosing your outfit for a first date also involves attending to the quality of your experience: you stop, look in the mirror, see how what you see hits you. A lot else might be going on—you might try to second-guess how your date may react and how their reaction might be different from yours. But whatever you do, it must involve attending to the relation between the object and the quality of your experience of the object.

Similarly, you spend hours climbing to a mountaintop. You finally look around. Sure, you'll attend to the view—the fields and rivers below. But not just that. If that's all you were attending to, it would not have been worth spending all that time on the climb. You will also attend to your own experience, which might be coloured by a sense of accomplishment.

How about Danièle Huillet's insistence that the experience she wants to trigger is one of absorption and not open-endedness or detachment? Absorption does not mean that the experience of what we are absorbed in completely falls out of the picture. When we are absorbed, we are often very much aware of being absorbed—we are enjoying not just what absorbs our attention but also the absorbed experience itself. So it is another way of attending to the relation between what we perceive and the experience of what we perceive.

While the importance of open-ended attention in aesthetic experience might be a specifically 'Western' thing, attending to the relation between the perceived object and the quality of the experience of this object is a theme we can find in a number of non-'Western' aesthetic traditions. One strikingly explicit example is Rasa: the central concept of Sanskrit aesthetics, which influenced thinking about art not only in India, but also in Indonesia and even parts of East Africa.

Rasa is often translated as the savouring of the emotional flavour of our experience. Flavour here is more than a metaphor—the experience of art in this tradition is a multimodal experience addressing all of our sense modalities. But the crucial point for our purposes is in the concept of 'savouring'. Savouring a meal means that you attend to the relation between the contrast and harmony of different experiences. It means attending to how different flavours hit you. In the example of forcing down the leftover Chinese food, this is exactly what was missing. Rasa theory takes something like what I referred to as aesthetic attention to be one of the most important components of our experience of works of art.

But one might wonder whether this would make aesthetic experience too cheap: I can attend to the quality of my experience while I am having my wisdom tooth extracted. I really can. And I can also attend to the relation between the tooth and my pain. But this does not make this experience an aesthetic experience (alas). What is also needed is the open-endedness of this attention.

And now we can put together the pieces of the puzzle about what makes aesthetic experiences aesthetic: the way we exercise our attention. It is a specific exercise of attention that could be described as seeing something as beautiful. And attention can be (but does not have to be) modulated by emotions.

We learned from the 'for its own sake' account about the importance of detachment and open-endedness in the aesthetic domain and we can do justice to this in terms of the free and open-ended attention with few no-go zones. And we have seen that the pleasure account owes us an theory of aesthetic attention—and this is exactly what I have tried to give here.

Finally, it's time to return to the question of sex, drugs, and rock 'n' roll. In the case of many sexual experiences we are attending to the relation between what we perceive and the quality of our experiences and the same goes for drugs (Huxley's vivid description of his peyote trips is all about this). So we have no reason to deny the aesthetic label from these experiences.

A recurring theme in old and by now somewhat stale discussions of perception is that perception is transparent. This just means that we see through our experience in the way we see through a clean window. The classic line is that if you are staring at a tomato and try to attend to your experience of the tomato, you automatically start attending to the tomato itself. So the experience itself is transparent—you look through it.

This may or may not be the case when you look at a tomato because you want to eat it. My claim is that things are very different when it comes to an aesthetic experience of a tomato. In this case, you attend not just to the tomato, but also to the quality of your experience of the tomato. And to the relation between the two. Aesthetic experiences are not transparent.

Chapter 4
Aesthetics and the self

Why do we pay a lot of money to listen to a concert or to buy a book? Why do we spend hours cooking a gourmet meal? And why do we exert a lot of energy to climb to a mountaintop? My answer is that we do all these things in order to have experiences that are important for us personally. These experiences matter for who we are, for who we take ourselves to be.

Just how important? Some recent experimental studies show that most of us consider our taste in music and film to be one of our most essential features. Our taste in food and clothing is not far behind. Imagine that tomorrow you wake up but you're much smarter than you are now. Or much less smart. Would that still be you? Or imagine that you wake up being kinder or skinnier or a Republican or less interested in yoga. Would that still be you?

According to the findings, very few of these compare to the scenario where you wake up and your musical taste is the exact opposite of what it used to be. We tend to consider our taste in music to be a way more important part of who we are than our moral, political, or even religious views.

Changing self, changing aesthetics

Our taste in music, film, and art is super-important for us. And not just that, our taste in what we eat, what kind of coffee we drink, how we dress. We take our aesthetic preferences to be a big part of who we are.

But these preferences change surprisingly quickly and often without us noticing. According to some recent findings aesthetic preferences are the most stable in middle-aged people and they are much more fluid in younger and, somewhat surprisingly, older age groups. But even the aesthetic preferences of people in the most stable age group undergo at least one major change as often as every two weeks in an aesthetic domain they really care about.

We like to think that we don't change much. Or if we do, we are in control of this change. But we are spectacularly wrong about this. We have very little control over how and how much we change.

Take the example of a widely explored psychological phenomenon, the 'mere exposure effect'. The more you are exposed to something, the more you tend to like it. Just the mere exposure to something changes your preferences. And this happens even if you are not aware of what you are exposed to.

The mere exposure effect influences your liking of people, songs, colours, even paintings. In one experiment, a professor of psychology at Cornell put some seemingly random pictures among the slides for an introductory vision science lecture. So in the middle of a lecture on how vision works you suddenly saw a Renoir or Morisot painting, with no explanation given. It was just there as decoration.

While these paintings seemed to come up randomly, they were part of an experiment. Some of them were shown more often than

Aesthetics

others and at the end of the semester, the students were asked to rate the pictures shown. They systematically rated those that were shown more often more highly than the ones that were shown only once. Very few of these students said that they remembered seeing any of these pictures before.

The mere exposure effect happens even if you are not aware of this exposure. An important set of findings about the mere exposure effect is that even unconscious exposure increases the probability of positive appraisal—say, if the stimulus is flashed for a very short time (under 200 milliseconds) or if the stimulus is masked (that is, cleverly hidden). It is hard not to be slightly upset by these findings. We have some control over what kinds of music and art we are exposed to, but definitely not complete control. It is more and more difficult to be in any kind of public space without music. Cafés, shopping malls, elevators. The music you are exposed to in these places leaves its mark on your preferences and this is very rarely something we would be happy about.

Our aesthetic preferences in music, film, food, clothing, and art are super-important for us, and they can and do change in a way that we have no control over. If you are a fan of free jazz and you think of yourself as a free jazz person, being exposed to Justin Bieber's music in the supermarket will make you like the particular musical style of Justin Bieber's songs a little bit more. And you are very likely to have no idea about this. It happens under the radar.

If our preferences can be hijacked without us noticing, then a big part of who we are seems to be the product of random mere exposure. And we are defenceless against this. When I was young and pretentious, I made a point of always walking through the pop art rooms in museums with my eyes closed. But this is difficult (and a little bit dangerous) to pull off. And when it comes to music, even more difficult. Our taste changes and there is not much we can do about it. The mere fact that it is difficult not to find this disconcerting shows just how important the aesthetic domain is for the self. But then we can't ignore this strong link between aesthetics and the self.

Experience versus judgement

Much of 'Western' aesthetics has been about well-informed aesthetic judgements. Aesthetic judgements are statements (often only to yourself, but sometimes also to others) that a particular object is beautiful or graceful or ugly or disgusting. But the vast majority of our aesthetic engagement is nothing like this. If it were, it would be difficult to explain why we care so much about all things aesthetic. The reason why we watch a three-hour-long film or take a day-long hike in the mountains is not to come up with a well-informed aesthetic judgement about the film or the landscape. If we take the importance of aesthetics in our life seriously, we need to shift the emphasis away from aesthetic judgements to forms of aesthetic engagement that are more enjoyable, more rewarding, and happen to us more often.

We do not go to a concert or cook for hours in order to pronounce aesthetic judgements. It is difficult to see why aesthetic judgements would matter for us that much. Making aesthetic judgements is really not that much fun, nor is it particularly rewarding. When we do take some kind of pleasure in making aesthetic judgements (say, when we rank our five favourite books or films, to post it on social media), this pleasure may have more to do with the communication of this judgement than with actually making the judgement. The same goes for long and intense debates with your friends about a film after seeing it in the cinema.

The temporal unfolding of our experiences in aesthetic contexts is, in contrast, fun, rewarding, and something we personally care about. It sometimes, but definitely not always, reaches its end point in an aesthetic judgement, but that is not why we are doing it. A major advantage of focusing on experiences and not on judgements is that it can help us understand the personal importance and urgency of all things aesthetic for the self.

But what is aesthetic judgement supposed to be? You go to the museum and look at a painting. You sit down in front of it and spend twenty minutes looking at it. Then you get up having formed an aesthetic judgement about it. And then you can communicate this aesthetic judgement to your friends or blog about it. Your experience of the painting lasts for twenty minutes. The judgement typically happens at the end of this process (although of course you can make judgements during the process, which you might revise later). 'Western' aesthetics has mainly focused on the judgement at the end of this process, not on the twenty-minute-long temporal unfolding of the experience (with its shifts of attention, visual comparisons, etc).

Aesthetic judgements don't even happen every time we engage with something aesthetically. It is an optional feature. Suppose that I spend twenty minutes in front of the painting but I just can't make up my mind about its aesthetic merits and demerits—I suspend judgement. This does not make my aesthetic engagement with the work of art any less rewarding or meaningful—or any less pleasurable. In fact, it can sometimes make your experience more pleasurable.

A lot has been said about how aesthetic judgements differ from other kinds of judgements. According to a broadly Kantian view, aesthetic judgement might not just be the end point of the experience; it might happen throughout and colour our experience itself. But even in this seemingly more experience-centred picture what matters most is the judgement. As long as we make the right judgement, it can lead us to have the right kind of experience. As we have seen extensively in Chapter 3, attention can change our experience radically. But aesthetic judgement very rarely can. Just because I believe that the picture is beautiful or graceful, my experience of it will be very unlikely to change (let alone change for the better). Attending to various thus far unnoticed features, in contrast, can change my experience significantly.

If we hold that aesthetics should be primarily concerned with the way our experience of the work of art unfolds temporally (whether or not this temporal unfolding culminates in an aesthetic judgement), then this general picture which begins with aesthetic judgements is just the wrong way of proceeding. We should not grant the assumption that we know the building blocks of all things aesthetic just because they are the building blocks of aesthetic judgements. We should examine our aesthetic engagement or experience in its own right and without borrowing any conceptual apparatus from the domain of aesthetic judgements.

Aesthetic experiences of our youth

Here is a striking demonstration of how the importance of aesthetics has little to do with our well-informed aesthetic judgement. Remember your very first strong aesthetic experience? As a child or maybe as a teenager? Some piece of music that just blew you away? A landscape that left you breathless? Here are three examples from my own life—feel free to change the examples to the ones from your youth.

Exhibit A: I was 16, standing in the old Tate Gallery (there was no Tate Modern then), mesmerized by a Clyfford Still painting. I must have spent two hours in front of it there and then. I didn't know much about Clyfford Still (1904–80) at that time. I knew he was an abstract expressionist, but that's about it. I loved the picture so much that the next day, when I was supposed to visit the Tower of London and the Houses of Parliament with my high school class, I left them, going back to Pimlico to have another look.

Exhibit B: rewind a year. I was so much into Michelangelo Antonioni's film *Blow-up* (1966) that I went to the cinema to see it two or three times a week. I knew the dialogues of the entire film by heart. Each time, I left the cinema in a state of rapture, of having understood something really important about love, appearance and reality, and other deep issues.

Exhibit C: rewind yet another year. I read a book that shook me to my core: Boris Vian's *L'Écume des jours* (1947). I had felt nothing like that ever before: I felt like laughing and crying at the same time.

The point I want to make is this: I now take *Blow-up* to be Antonioni's single worst film. *L'Écume des jours* is full of references I had no chance of understanding at age 14 and it's way less original than some of Vian's other novels. I still think that Clyfford Still is great, but there are also many other great works of art in that collection where, for some reason, I fell in love with this painting.

I went to Tate Modern just yesterday, in preparation for writing this chapter to see how I reacted. Well, not very strongly. I also watched *Blow-up* again (on my laptop, as cinemas don't seem to show Antonioni films any more), but I had to switch it off after twenty minutes or so, I just couldn't be bothered. And I put down the English translation of *L'Écume des jours* after a couple of pages (to be fair, it was because of the translation).

I had a much stronger and more rewarding aesthetic experience of these works of art when I first encountered them, knowing very little about art history, film history, or the history of 20th-century French literature than I do now, when I know a little more. I want to think that I am in a better position now to assess the aesthetic value of these works than I was at age 14–16. I can make a better aesthetic judgement now. But it is not as enthusiastic as it was then.

With my 20/20 hindsight, I should condemn the aesthetic judgement of the 14–16-year-old Bence, shouldn't I? But if I hadn't felt so strongly about these artworks, I would probably not have taken an interest in the arts and so wouldn't have picked up all the knowledge that now allows me to patronize the teenage Bence.

What would be a well-informed aesthetic judgement here? Take the judgement I just made about *Blow-up* being Antonioni's single worst film. That is the kind of judgement aesthetics should be about—we are told. The kind of liking I took in *Blow-up* as a 15-year-old is not what aesthetics is about.

My examples were intended to show that there can be, and there often is, a mismatch between the maturity of aesthetic judgements and the strength of our aesthetic experience. One conclusion that follows from this is that focusing exclusively on well-informed aesthetic judgements would leave something really important out of discussions of aesthetics: that aesthetic engagement is pleasurable and that it has some personal importance for us. We care about aesthetic engagement. An exclusive focus on well-informed aesthetic judgement cannot do justice to this very simple fact about aesthetics.

The primacy of experience

There is an even more important reason why I introduced these examples. We have seen that it is not the case that the better informed our aesthetic judgement is, the stronger or more rewarding our aesthetic experience gets. One consequence of this is that we should include strong, rewarding, and personally important aesthetic experiences in the discussion of aesthetics (and not sacrifice these for the exclusive focus on aesthetic judgements). But experiences are also prior to judgements in a very different sense. Each and every one of our well-informed aesthetic judgements relies on some earlier experiences that are rewarding, personally important to us, and not at all well informed.

When you step into a room with many paintings in a museum and take a quick look around, maybe you like some of the pictures on display, but not others. You have no idea who painted which picture, so any well-informed judgement is out of the question. But it is this initial liking that determines which painting you will approach and spend more time exploring. The only reason we are in the position to make all things considered well-informed aesthetic judgements is because we took a liking to some artworks earlier—maybe just seconds ago, or decades ago, and that's why we're engaging with this artwork and not some other one.

Let's take a step back. We have two instances of aesthetic engagement here. The experience I had as a teenager (very positive, very rewarding, very important for me personally) and the judgement I am making now (judging the work somewhat mediocre, not very rewarding, no importance for me personally). The latter is what we call a well-informed aesthetic judgement. And the latter could not have happened without the former. The question is this: what explains the aesthetic pleasure of the earlier aesthetic engagement? If we restrict our discussion to aesthetic judgements, it is difficult to see how we can answer this question. It can't be the maturity of our aesthetic judgement because the earlier aesthetic judgement was not at all mature or well informed. Maybe the strong and rewarding earlier experience was completely inadequate and aesthetically irrelevant, but then it would seem that inadequate and aesthetically irrelevant responses are largely responsible for our aesthetic preferences, as my current aesthetic preferences are very much a product of those aesthetic experiences of teenage Bence.

This is not a trivial problem. Here is one way of making it more urgent: why should I care about my well-informed aesthetic judgements if they leave me cold? They neither give me any pleasure nor are they of any personal importance to me. Why should we learn more about art history and the history of 20th-century French literature if the result is that we have less fun engaging with art?

Here is one way out of this conundrum. Aesthetic judgements are not that much fun. Neither the naive one of the kind I made as a teenager nor the well-informed one I am making now. Making judgements, in general, is rarely rewarding or entertaining or pleasurable. Experiences, on the other hand, can very much be rewarding or entertaining or pleasurable. Similarly, pronouncing judgements is rarely the kind of thing we find personally meaningful. Experiences are the kind of things we find personally meaningful. So aesthetics should be about experiences, not judgement. These experiences can lead to judgement, which we can communicate to others and that's a nice optional add-on, but they do not need to lead to judgement.

We spend so much time and money engaging with works of art not because we want to make aesthetic judgements about them. We do it because the experience we have while engaging with works of art can be pleasurable, rewarding, and personally meaningful. Not the judgement—the experience.

We should try to move away from the concept of aesthetic judgement in general—whether or not it is well informed. The aim of aesthetic engagement with an artwork is very rarely to come up with an aesthetic judgement and our aesthetic theory should respect this fact. We should focus on the temporal unfolding of our aesthetic experience and not on the (clearly optional) end point of pronouncing aesthetic judgements. As Susan Sontag said: 'A work of art encountered as a work of art is an experience, not a statement or an answer to a question.'

Why judgements?

In order to shift the emphasis of aesthetic theory from aesthetic judgement to the temporal unfolding of aesthetic engagement, we need to understand why aestheticians are obsessed with aesthetic judgements to begin with.

One reason is clearly historical. The key concept of 'Western' aesthetics has always been that of aesthetic judgement, at least since David Hume's 'Of the Standard of Taste' (1757)—which was published more than 250 years ago.

Hume (1711–76), whose influence on Anglo-American philosophical aesthetics is difficult to overstate, explicitly talks about the differences between the ways two different people make judgements of taste. He gives the following story as an illustration (borrowed from *Don Quixote*). Two people drink from the same wine and are asked to judge its quality. One of them says it has a discernible odd leathery taste. The other one thinks it has an unpleasant metallic note. The punchline of Hume's story is that while we might think that at least one of these judgements is just plain wrong, when the wine was inspected, they discovered a small key with a leather thong attached. So they were both right.

I will come back to this story in Chapter 5. But what matters for us now is that although Hume clearly stresses the importance of perceptual discrimination here, what he mainly cares about is the aesthetic judgement of these two wine connoisseurs. It does not matter for them how their experience of wine unfolded through time (although a lot can be said about how the experience of wine unfolds over time). The only thing that matters is the aesthetic judgement they came up with—and how the two judgements are related to one another.

As we shall see in Chapter 5, there are important philosophical reasons why Hume was focusing on judgements, but the strength of his influence on the field of aesthetics meant that his assumption that the central concern of aesthetics is understanding aesthetic judgements went unquestioned.

Another important historical reason for the dominance of judgements in aesthetics has to do with the strong influence of philosophy of language on philosophy in general and aesthetics in particular. Aesthetic judgements are statements (that we make to ourselves or to others) that philosophy of language has a lot to say about. So aesthetic judgement is a familiar subject for aestheticians with strong philosophy of language training. Experiences, in contrast, are not so easy to analyse using the conceptual toolkit of philosophy of language.

Going global

Here it is difficult not to point to the idiosyncrasy of this judgement-centred perspective if we broaden the scope of what we take to be aesthetics from strictly 'Western' aesthetics to global aesthetics. The vast majority of aesthetic traditions outside the 'West' are not too concerned with aesthetic judgements at all. They are concerned with the way our emotions unfold, the way our perception is altered, and the way aesthetic engagement interacts with social engagement.

The most extreme example comes from Islamic aesthetics (and especially Islamic aesthetics in the Sufi tradition). One way in which Islamic aesthetics is different from the aesthetic traditions of the 'West' is in its emphasis on the ever-changing nature of the world in general and of our experience of artworks in particular. And part of what is special about the engagement with art is our appreciation of these ever-changing, flickering experiences (an example would be the deliberately different views certain architectural features offer as we move around them, often further underlined by their fleeting reflections in water). This tradition is very much interested in beauty, but not with judgements about beauty, rather with the ways in which beauty could be explained in terms of the working of our perceptual system. And its emphasis on the ever-changing, flickering nature of our experience makes any attempt at a fixed judgement impossible.

Aesthetics

We have also seen how Rasa theory is about the savouring of our multimodal emotional experiences, not judgements, which Rasa theory hardly talks about. On the rare occasion when what we would call aesthetic judgement is mentioned in Rasa theory, it is to show how stable and inflexible judgements would in fact work *against* this savouring of our experience. Finally, to give a somewhat obscure example, in Assyro-Babylonian aesthetics, the key concept of Tabritu is often translated as admiration and awe, but it is very clearly identified as the perceptual experience of the work, which involves 'repeated and continuous looking'—again, unfolding experience, not judgement. The fact that in our 'Western' tradition aesthetic judgement has played such an important role is little more than a historical curiosity.

A less historical, but more substantial reason why the concept of aesthetic judgement has dominated 'Western' aesthetics is that aesthetic judgements are communicable. When we have aesthetic disagreements, we have disagreements about aesthetic judgements: I say that the film was bad, you say it was good. So in order to understand the intersubjective and social aspects of our engagement with works, the argument would go, we need to focus on aesthetic judgements. The subject of Chapter 5 is this interpersonal dimension of aesthetics.

Chapter 5
Aesthetics and the other

Aesthetics is rarely a solitary endeavour. We share meals, we go to the museum with our friends, and we choose furniture for our flat together. When we go to a concert or to the cinema, we are in a room full of people who are having very similar experiences to ours. We are social beings and there are very few aesthetic situations that are devoid of all social aspects.

Further, it can be an important link between two friends if they have similar experiences when listening to the same song. And it can be alienating if your friend has a terrible experience while you have a mind-blowing one, while you both watch the same movie.

Aesthetic agreements and disagreements

It is somewhat unfortunate that the discussion of the social dimension of aesthetics in the history of 'Western' aesthetics has been dominated by one question and one question only: that of aesthetic agreements and disagreements.

Who is the better composer: Johnny Rotten or Wolfgang Amadeus Mozart? The intuition to be pumped here is that Mozart is the better one, everybody knows that. There is complete aesthetic agreement on this. And if there isn't, there should be. Those who prefer Johnny Rotten should know better. They should listen to more Mozart and then they will see the error of their ways.

In some sense the Johnny Rotten vs Mozart comparison is silly. There are probably very few heated late night arguments where one person (seriously) takes the side of Johnny Rotten and the other one defends Mozart. But we do very often argue about aesthetic matters—in fact, this is one of the most important things we argue about. Bach or Handel? Frida Kahlo or Diego Rivera? Or if these seem too highbrow, Beatles or Rolling Stones? *Seinfeld* or *Arrested Development*? Which *Fast & Furious* film? But also, to move away from art: is Han Solo or Luke Skywalker the more attractive? Is Paris prettier than Barcelona? Dark roast or light roast for coffee beans? Is steak better rare or medium rare? And so on.

Here are two obvious options for settling disagreements of this kind. We can agree to disagree. You like this, I like that. Neither of us is right, or, rather, we are both right. The other option is that one of us is just dead wrong. The plausibility of these two options will depend on which examples we pick. The Johnny Rotten vs Mozart case is a cheap shot at giving support to the second option. And the Frida Kahlo or Diego Rivera example could be seen as supporting the first one.

Compare aesthetic disagreements to disagreements about more prosaic things. If we both look at a painting, and I say it's square shaped, while you say it's triangle shaped, (at least) one of us is just mistaken. But if we look at the same painting and we disagree about its aesthetic qualities, things are less clear.

Another comparison would be with clearly 'subjective' disagreements. If we look at the same painting and I say it reminds me of my grandmother and you say it does not remind you of your grandmother, then these two opinions are consistent with each other (even if we have the same grandmother). I'm right and you are also right.

The question is whether aesthetic disagreement is closer to the 'square vs triangle' disagreement or to the 'reminds me of my grandmother or not' disagreement. And some of the central texts of 'Western' aesthetics tried to carve out an intermediate position between the purely 'subjective' disagreement (like the one involving my grandmother) and the purely 'objective' disagreement (like the one involving shapes).

Remember Hume's iron key with leather thong story? The reason why he gave this parable is exactly to tackle the problem of aesthetic agreements and disagreements. The two wine experts disagree. One discerns an iron taste, the other a leathery one. But it turns out that both are right. They are both right, but not because the judgement of taste is entirely 'subjective', but because there is an 'objective' basis for their judgement of taste: the key with the leather thong. But if a third expert had joined the party saying that the wine tastes of sulphur, she would be just mistaken. Judgements of taste are more restricted than judgements about what reminds me of my grandmother, but less restricted than judgements about shapes.

Aesthetics is not for policing

At this point of the aesthetic disagreement debate, one long and suspicious word invariably makes an appearance: normativity. The idea is that aesthetic evaluations have some kind of normative force. We *should* make certain kinds of judgement when appreciating certain objects. If we don't make these kinds of judgement, we err: we're not doing what we're supposed to be doing.

The general thought is that the domain of aesthetics is similar to the domain of morality in this respect: both are about what we should do and not about what we in fact do. Ethics tells us whether we should lie or steal or become vegetarians. And aesthetics tells us what kinds of aesthetic experiences we should have and when.

Normativity is about what we should do. And many aspects of our aesthetic life are very much normative in some respects. I myself have been making, and will continue to make, a fairly normative claim about how aesthetics should not privilege the 'West'. And it would be difficult to talk about some well-established aesthetic practices without making at least some normative claims about what, for example, performers of a musical piece *should* do for their performance to count as a performance *of* a certain musical piece (and not just of random notes). The word 'should' pops up all over the place when we talk about the aesthetic domain (and it pops up all over the place in this book as well).

Nonetheless, and I can't stress this strongly enough, aesthetics is not a normative discipline. Some parts of ethics might really be about normative claims (well, a branch of ethics is called 'normative ethics', so that would be a good candidate). But aesthetics is not. Aesthetics is not primarily about what we should do. It is about what we in fact do in what circumstances.

You might expect a work in ethics to convince you about whether you should become vegetarian or keep on eating meat. But you should not expect any works in aesthetics to give you that kind of advice. Aesthetics is not trying to tell you what you should do—which works of art you should admire and which ones to ignore. This way of thinking about aesthetics could go a long way towards dispelling the strong mistrust towards aesthetics as a discipline among many artists, who often feel that aesthetics is telling them what they are allowed to do and what they are not allowed to do and, more importantly, what kind of reaction is appropriate to their works.

Some branches of ethics might be about policing your behaviour in moral matters. But aesthetics is not about policing your aesthetic responses. Your aesthetic responses are what they are and you should not let anybody police them. As a result, we should view any appearance of words like normativity in aesthetics with great suspicion.

And this also goes for words like 'normativity' in the aesthetic disagreements debate. The general thought here is that aesthetic judgements or aesthetic evaluations have 'normative force'. This can mean many things. It can mean that your aesthetic reaction may be correct or incorrect. If you like works that are not to be liked, you're just wrong. If you dislike masterworks, you are wrong again. You *should* have a certain emotional or aesthetic reaction in the face of a certain work. If you don't, your aesthetic reaction is not what it should be. You are *wrong* to have this reaction.

If you don't like the authoritarian overtones of this line of thinking about the aesthetic, it is important to realize that this picture is deeply rooted in a very special (and very 'West'-centred) way of thinking about aesthetics. It is easy to see how we can make normative claims about aesthetic judgements. Judgements can be right or wrong and they are often wrong. But if we are interested in experiences, not judgements, then how could we even formulate normative claims? Here is an attempt. While experiences can't be right or wrong, they can be accurate or inaccurate. Perceptual illusions are inaccurate, for example. Just as you could misperceive the colour of an object, because it is too dark, you could also have an illusory aesthetic experience.

Crucially, this line of argument only works if we subscribe to what I labelled the beauty-salon approach to aesthetics: the view that what makes an experience aesthetic is that it is about beautiful things and that there is a hard division-line between beautiful things and non-beautiful things. When we have an inaccurate aesthetic experience, we experience a beautiful thing as non-beautiful (or a non-beautiful thing as beautiful).

But we have seen that the beauty-salon approach to aesthetics is not exactly an attractive view. What makes an experience aesthetic is not that it is about a beautiful thing. What makes it aesthetic is the way you exercise your attention. And there is no accurate or inaccurate way of exercising your attention. So while experiences may be accurate or illusory, what makes them aesthetic has nothing to do with their accuracy. It has everything to do with the way attention is exercised.

Let us go back to the aesthetic disagreements debate. The question there is about whether aesthetic disagreements are more like disagreements about the shape of the painting (you say triangle, I say square) or like disagreements about whether it reminds me of my grandmother. But even formulating this question takes for granted the beauty-salon approach to aesthetics.

If what matters for aesthetic engagement has little to do with the features attributed to the perceived object, then the comparison with disagreements about other attributed features, like shapes and whether it reminds me of my grandmother, are meaningless.

When you and I are looking at the same artwork or the same landscape, my experience might be very different from yours. But framing this difference as a disagreement either sneaks in an emphasis on aesthetic judgements (rather than experiences) or it commits us to the beauty-salon approach wholesale.

It matters for us if you and I have different experiences in front of the same artwork or landscape. It matters much more than a disagreement about shapes or about what reminds whom of their grandmother. And dumbing down the social dimension of aesthetic engagement to aesthetic disagreements fails to appreciate just how crucial aesthetics is in our everyday life and everyday social interactions.

Just one, somewhat embarrassing, example. The social dimension of aesthetics seems especially important in one's youth, when we tend to hang out with people who like the same music and despise others who like different music, for example. When I was in high school (and a huge snob, as we have seen in Chapter 4), I spent a summer in Germany allegedly learning German. I really liked one of the German girls and she really liked me and our budding relationship after various outings took us to her place. The first thing I remember seeing there was a giant Eros Ramazzotti poster, as she was a fan of this particular Italian pop singer.

There was a blatant aesthetic disagreement right there—let's just say that I was not one of Eros Ramazzotti's fans. But I powered through that little blip. It was when she dimmed the light and put on an Eros Ramazzotti CD in order to enhance the romantic mood that I just couldn't take it any more. Difference of opinion about aesthetic matters was OK. But when it came to being forced to have a shared romantic experience of Eros Ramazzotti's timbre, that was over the line.

Aesthetic disagreements matter, no doubt about that. But sharing or failing to share aesthetic experiences matters much more. And there are no right or wrong ways of having aesthetic experiences.

This does not mean that anything goes in aesthetics. Some artworks clearly try to evoke very specific reactions and if you have the opposite reaction, then something went astray. Suppose that you are sitting in front of your favourite painting in a museum. You are failing to have the experience you know that you could, and in some sense should, have in front of the painting in the museum. You are failing in an important sense, but this is not some kind of failing that needs to be policed.

As we have seen, we can change someone's aesthetic experience by drawing her attention to certain features. This is a much better way of dealing with differences of experience than cracking down on deviant ones. Lack of policing does not lead to anarchy. If we are lucky, it leads to conversation, peaceful coexistence, and diversity.

Back to normativity and its abuses. A more modest, but not at all less harmful, appeal to normativity, is about the universal appeal of aesthetic evaluations. It is not that a certain artwork just demands you to have a certain aesthetic reaction. Rather, when you have an aesthetic reaction, you implicitly assume that everybody else has, or at least should have, the same reaction. This is Immanuel Kant's view and it has had a lasting influence on 'Western' aesthetics.

I'm trying to say this politely and in awe of the intellectual achievement of Kant's philosophy, but this is one of the most arrogant ideas in the history of aesthetics. If you implicitly assume that everybody else should have the same reaction as you do, then you seriously underappreciate the diversity of humankind and the diversity of the cultural backgrounds people come from. And any time we are even tempted to think (or assume or feel) that whatever we do has universal appeal or universal communicability, that would be a good time to stop and exercise what I call 'aesthetic humility'—thinking about just how contingent our own position and cultural background is compared to the vast diversity of cultures on this planet. I will return to these themes in Chapter 7.

Aesthetic disagreements in real life

The real question about aesthetic agreements and disagreements is not about who is right and who is wrong. It is about the ways in which our experiences depend on the allocation of our attention, our background beliefs and knowledge as well as our past exposure. Knowing how these can alter our experience can help a lot in resolving aesthetic disagreements.

I used to work as a film critic. One of the better aspects of the job was to go to film festivals where I was often one of the jury members. Being on a jury at a film festival has its glamorous side—meeting famous actors and actresses, staying in fancy hotels, and so on. But it was also sometimes an exhausting and often infuriating experience.

You sit on a jury with four other people who are often from very different parts of the world and have very different taste in film from yours. But you need to come to some kind of decision about which film should get the prize. And there is always a strict deadline for doing so. You have to give the festival organizers a title by midnight. It's already 11 pm and there is no agreement about any of the films whatsoever. This is aesthetic disagreement in real life and resolving this disagreement is a task that Hume is not exactly helping with. After serving on juries a couple of times, the stale debates about aesthetic disagreement started to look very different to me.

What is going on in these jury meetings is not about sharing experiences, it is about hard aesthetic judgements. We had to agree that one film is better than the others. In fact, the way it actually worked was usually the other way round. First, we had to agree that some films would clearly not win the prize. This was the easier part. But then we were left with four or five remaining films and that's when the knives came out.

How do you try to convince another critic rationally that the film she liked was in fact derivative and clichéd? I'm afraid that the answer is that you don't and you can't. There was nothing rational about these debates. And, sadly, often the prize went to a film that none of the critics were crazy about, but that all of us could live with as the prizewinner.

The convincing was not rational—and I have seen very few critics trying to be rational. (Some more experienced critics were experimenting with some form of psychological warfare, systematically undermining, and sometimes unconsciously priming against, some films well before the jury discussion, and often during the screening. This psychological warfare was not rational either, but fought on a more emotional level. But I'm not sure much is to be learned from this for aesthetics in general other than the deviousness of critics...)

Almost the only thing that happened on these juries was trying to get other critics to attend to certain features of the films. This is not as obvious as it would be in the case of judging paintings or novels as film is a temporal art. We were days after having seen some of these films and what we could attend to was not the film itself, but rather our recollection of the film.

Nonetheless, almost all the arguments were really ways of directing the other critics' attention to some thus far unnoticed feature. Attending to this feature could make a negative aesthetic difference—when the aim was to dismiss this film. But it could also make a positive aesthetic difference—an argument for why this film is better than the rest of the field.

And this is in fact what critics should do, not only when they are on the jury, but also when they write reviews. This is what good critics actually do. Not treating criticism as an art form, as Pauline Kael (1919–2001), the iconic American film critic, did. Not summarizing the plot. Not telling their childhood memories very loosely connected to the plot. Not telling us what they liked and what they didn't. The critic's job is to direct our attention to features we would not have noticed otherwise. Attending to some of these features can completely transform our experience.

Some of these features may be structural—for example, how a theme on page 12 of the novel returns on page 134 and then again

on page 432 and 563, and how this gives a structure to the
otherwise unstructured narrative. Some others may be about links
to other works of art—how a musical work quotes a tune from
another musical work, for example. Attending to some of these
features might make our experience more rewarding. And that
makes reading critics actually worth the effort.

Here is a real-life example: a small painting from 15th-century
Italy, depicting the Annunciation (Figure 4). The painter
(Domenico Veneziano, *c*.1410–1461) had a little fun with the axes
of symmetry: the symmetrical building is off-centre—it's pushed
to the left of the middle of the picture. And the 'action' is also
off-centre—but it is pushed to the right, not to the left. Attending
to the interplay between these three axes of symmetry (of the
building, of the picture itself, and of the axis halfway between
Mary and the archangel) is not something everybody notices
immediately. But when it is pointed out and your attention is
drawn to it, this can make a huge aesthetic difference.

In terms of sheer quantity, there has never been as much criticism
as there is today with literally hundreds of thousands of blogs and
websites. But this just makes it even more obvious that criticism is
in crisis. As Terry Eagleton (1943–), the British literary critic,
eloquently put it more than thirty years ago (way before blogs),
'criticism today lacks all substantive social function. It is either
part of the public relations branch of the literary industry, or a
matter wholly internal to the academies.' One thing that has
changed since then is the emergence of the celebrity critic who
opines about films, music, and TV shows (often in front of live
audiences) without doing much else. But the social function of
criticism can be restored if critics just do what they are paid to do,
namely, guide the reader's attention to features that could make
an aesthetic difference.

André Malraux (1901–76), the French novelist, said that the
primary aim of writing about art is not to enable the reader to

4. Domenico Veneziano, *Annunciation* (15th century), Fitzwilliam Museum, Cambridge.

understand art, but to persuade her to love it. Pontificating about art is of course much easier, but the critic is only doing her job if she helps the reader attend to the work in a way that persuades her to love it.

Aesthetic agreements in real life

Another important lesson I learned from being on the jury at film festivals was, oddly, not about aesthetic disagreements, but about aesthetic agreements. I found myself agreeing again and again with some critics in spite of the fact that they were from completely different continents and often they were fifty or so years my senior. And this made me wonder about what it is that explains this convergence between the aesthetic evaluations of a 20-something Hungarian living in the US and, say, a 70-something Argentinian living in Hong Kong.

And what I noticed more and more often is that these critics and I grew up watching very similar films. We liked the same films from the festival offering because we were primed to like them by the films we watched as teenagers. This was a hunch then, but as it turns out, there are some hard psychological findings that support this hunch.

As we have seen, the mere exposure effect is the well-known phenomenon that repeated previous exposure to a stimulus makes the positive appraisal of this stimulus more likely and this effect is also present in the aesthetic domain. But there is an important distinction to be made between two different kinds of mere exposure findings. The experiment I mentioned in Chapter 4 (about the Cornell professor showing slides with seemingly random impressionist paintings during class) was about how being exposed to one *specific painting* makes you like *that painting* more. But other mere exposure findings are about how input *of a certain kind* makes you like input *of that kind* more. So seeing many impressionist paintings could make you like another impressionist painting—one you have never seen before—more. And this means that the kind of artworks you have seen before deeply influence what kinds of artworks you will like.

If you watched 1960s black-and-white formalist French and Italian films in your formative years, then you will like films that resemble those in some broad manner (in their composition or maybe in their narrative). And this is true no matter whether you grew up in Budapest or in Buenos Aires.

The mere exposure effect may be even more salient in music: the kind of music you listened to in your formative years (which above all means early childhood and teenage exposure) will have a huge impact on what music you will be drawn to as an adult. Musical taste changes—it often changes radically. But that does not mean that your old favourites just get overwritten. They will always have an influence on what music you like.

In Chapter 4, I wrote about the worrying aspects of the mere exposure effect for just how unnoticeable the changes to our aesthetic preferences can be. But the mere exposure effect is not all bad. Knowing about how our aesthetic preferences are rooted in our very specific cultural and perceptual background can help us dial down our aesthetic arrogance and push us towards aesthetic humility.

Aesthetic humility

If you have listened to thrash metal since the age of 8, your aesthetic preferences are going to be very different from someone who grew up only listening to traditional Indonesian gamelan music. Nothing surprising so far. You will be sensitive to nuances that the gamelan fan will not even hear. You can attend to features in thrash metal that very few others will notice.

I will probably trust you and not my gamelan connoisseur friend if I want to figure out which Slayer album to listen to, because you will be a much more reliable source. But that is not the end of the story. The mere exposure to thrash metal will make you have aesthetic preferences for certain musical forms and rhythms that will probably colour your engagement with any other musical works.

Suppose I make both you and my gamelan friend listen to some early 20th-century Viennese atonal music or some seriously dissonant New York free jazz. You will both like some of these pieces and dislike others. But part of what makes you like this piece and not that one is your exposure to thrash metal. (I hope it is clear that I am not trying to dismiss thrash metal here—the same thing would happen if an atonally trained person listened to thrash metal for the first time.) And my gamelan-trained friend will like different pieces because of her mere exposure to gamelan music.

You might say that there is aesthetic disagreement here. But is there? What this example shows us is that we make aesthetic evaluations from the very specific perspective of our past exposure to certain works of art (and other stimuli). This does not mean that our past exposure fully determines our aesthetic evaluations. But it anchors these aesthetic evaluations and it will always show up in them. In this sense, all aesthetic evaluations are tied or indexed to the evaluator's cultural and perceptual background. Your evaluation of the atonal piece is tied to your thrash metal cultural background. My friend's evaluation of the very same piece is tied to her gamelan background.

It makes no sense to ask who is right and who is wrong. If aesthetic evaluations are indexed to the cultural background of the evaluator, then there is no actual aesthetic disagreement here, because you are making an evaluation indexed to a thrash metal cultural background and my gamelan friend is making an evaluation indexed to a very different cultural background.

This does not mean that there are no facts of the matter about aesthetic evaluation; it does not mean that anything goes when it comes to aesthetics. It just means that aesthetic evaluations are relative to the cultural background of the evaluators. If two evaluators have the very same cultural background and they disagree, this would indeed be a genuine aesthetic disagreement—one of them would be right and the other one wrong.

I made this thrash metal/atonal music example a bit extreme. Nobody listens to only one kind of music. Even if you are a huge thrash metal fan, you can't just filter out all other music (like that Justin Bieber at the mall). But this does not change the force of the argument that your aesthetic evaluations are a function of your cultural background. What follows from this is that you should be aware of your cultural background when making aesthetic evaluations. Your aesthetic evaluation is not some kind of universal standard. It is a very specific affair, deeply rooted in your very contingent cultural background. So we should treat all things aesthetic with a fair amount of humility.

Chapter 6
Aesthetics and life

Aesthetics is about special moments. But are these moments isolated islands in our otherwise dull daily routine? I don't think so. If you're lucky, you can have as many as three aesthetic experiences before breakfast.

But art as well as our engagements with all things aesthetic can also influence our life in a more prosaic manner. You dress like one of the characters in your favourite movie (probably without being aware of it), you use phrases you learn from sitcoms. And looking at photography helps people to see, as Berenice Abbot (1898–1991), the avant-garde photographer, says. Aesthetics and life are intertwined on all kinds of levels.

Life as a work of art?

The importance of the aesthetic for our life does not mean that we need to resort to cheap self-help slogans. One breathtakingly popular and influential such idea is that we should turn our life into—or treat our life as—a work of art. I want to make it clear how what I am saying is different from this.

Everyone who is anyone in 'Western' modernity endorsed some version of this metaphor, from Johann Wolfgang von Goethe (1749–1832) and Friedrich Nietzsche (1844–1990) to Marcel

Duchamp (1887–1968). So much so, that Robert Musil (1880–1942), the Austrian novelist, author of *The Man Without Qualities*, was having some fun stretching this line of self-help advice to its breaking point:

> What sort of life is it that one has to keep riddling with holes called 'holidays'? Would we punch holes in a painting because it demands too much from us in appreciation of the beautiful?

If you squint, you could see how this life as a work of art idea could make some kind of sense in the 19th century, when works of art were well-constructed coherent wholes. I can see someone striving to turn their life into a Jane Austen (1775–1817) novel, which has a beginning, a middle, and an end, in this order, and a nice coherent, and often moving, arc connecting these. But turning your life into a Marguerite Duras (1914–96) novel, where literally nothing happens, or a Roberto Bolaño (1953–2003) novel, where only terrible things happen, would be a very dubious enterprise.

The more general problem is that art has become too much like life. In fact, the big slogan of the art movements in the last half-century or so (at least since fluxus and pop art) has been that art should not be cut off from life. So if art becomes like life, then turning your life into a work of art either makes no sense or it is pure anachronism. There is even a sub-genre of visual art where the artist cuts actual holes into their pictures, which makes the Musil quote even funnier.

But maybe I'm not being charitable enough. Maybe the main idea here is not that our life should be turned into a work of art, but rather that our attitude towards life should be like our attitude towards a work of art.

This approach is not without its heroes either. Albert Camus (1913–60), in his largely forgotten novel *A Happy Death* (1938), writes that 'like all works of art, life also demands that we think about it'. A nice one-liner, but the reference to works of art is really a red herring. Lots of things demand that we think about them—philosophy books, news from the White House, the mystery of why Cinderella's shoe would fall off if it fitted her perfectly.

So works of art are not particularly helpful in this respect to compare life to. And while some works of art surely demand thinking about them, what kind of explicit thought would be appropriate as a response to the *Brandenburg Concertos* (1721) or a Mondrian painting? Camus's bon mot does not really add anything new to the old 'unexamined life not worth living' mantra.

Lots of things can be art. And there are lots of ways to relate to works of art, none of them are inherently better than others. So urging us to turn our life into a work of art—or to relate to life as if it were a work of art—is neither helpful nor particularly meaningful.

Spectators of our own life?

There is another popular way of connecting aesthetics and our life that I want to keep a safe distance from. In some ways it is a version of the treating your life as a work of art idea, but a very specific version. The gist is that the right attitude to have both towards life and towards works of art is to be detached spectators. As Oscar Wilde would put it, we should become the spectators of our own life.

This general idea was very influential in much of the 19th and 20th centuries. And many works of art created in the 'West' in the last couple of hundred years were clearly going for this effect. Many of the literary greats I cite in this book (from Pessoa to Proust) very clearly subscribe to this idea of aesthetic engagement. Even Susan Sontag, otherwise very discerning about sweeping claims concerning art, jumps on the bandwagon when she says that 'all great art induces contemplation, a dynamic contemplation'.

An advantage of taking the role of attention in aesthetic experience seriously is that we can explain why this kind of detached, contemplative experience has been a central metaphor but also how it is not a necessary feature of all aesthetic engagement. The kind of engagement Sontag, Proust, or Pessoa talk about can be characterized as open-ended attention roaming freely across the features of the artwork.

As we have seen, this way of exercising your attention accounts for a historically and geographically very specific form of aesthetic experience, which overlaps with the kind of experiences labelled as contemplation fairly well. But this is still just one kind of aesthetic experience, regardless of how influential it was in Europe in, say, the first half of the 20th century. Aesthetic experience does not have to be detached, it does not need to be contemplative, and it does not need to involve open-ended attention.

Many devotees of the idea of being spectators of our own life became very suspicious of this very concept in the light of the political events of the 1930s. The French novelist André Gide (1869–1951) wrote in his diary in 1934, a year after Hitler's rise to power, that 'whoever remains contemplative today demonstrates either an inhuman philosophy or monstrous blindness'.

More generally, the emphasis on contemplation seems to go against the undeniable political elements in art. Contemplation is often seen as apolitical, and choosing contemplation instead of political activity, in troubled times, is often regarded with suspicion.

And regardless of how we think about aesthetics, we should not automatically remove politics from the domain of aesthetics, nor should we remove aesthetics from the domain of politics. The emphasis on contemplation leads easily to some kind of sharp opposition of politics and aesthetics, but any such opposition would just be historically and psychologically inaccurate.

To the contrary, aesthetic actions have been, and still are, an important vehicle of political ideas. In fact, this is an important aspect of the social relevance of aesthetics. One of the most memorable aesthetic experiences of my youth was a demonstration against the Russian occupation of Hungary in 1988, when completely unexpectedly we could freely chant 'Russians go home' in a large crowd without having to fear a police crack-down. I really like Stendhal's take on this connection (which also emphasizes the concept of attention): 'in literary works politics is like a gunshot during a concert. It is a bit vulgar, but it does make everybody pay attention immediately.'

How about the contemplation of your own life? The idea that a good life means having a contemplative relation to our life goes hand in hand with the emphasis on contemplative aesthetic experiences. And it is easy to see how this is a line some more current self-help schools like the Stoic/Buddhist revival or mindfulness would exploit with a vengeance. We have seen that contemporary art has moved away from contemplation. And it is the diminishing role of contemplation in our artworld that made it so easy for the mindfulness industry to take over that niche.

The link between life and aesthetics is way more important and rewarding than just a platitude about contemplation. Aesthetic experiences can help us avoid being jaded. They can teach us new ways of seeing the world.

How not to be jaded

I talked about the philosophical lessons that being a film critic taught me. But being a film critic also has a pretty depressing side.

You have to spend a lot of time with other film critics, many of whom have been in the job for many decades.

Maybe I was unlucky, but I had to spend a lot of time with film critics who were incredibly jaded. They said (often and loudly) how much they loved film, but I saw very little trace of this. They complained about every single film we watched together, and even the ones they did not absolutely hate they only saw through the angle of what they could say about them at the prize deliberations or in their review.

The reason I gave up being a film critic and decided to live the much less glamorous life of an academic is that I didn't want to be like them. I did not want to become jaded. I did not want to forget how to be truly touched and moved and lifted by a film or by other works of art.

But what did these people do wrong? How did they become so jaded? Take one example: Ronnie (which may or may not be his real name). Ronnie was English—very English. He wrote for one of the top British newspapers, but he also had side-gigs in pretty much all of the quality print media of the United Kingdom. He was not young. He had spent his youth in Paris, hobnobbing in the literary and film scene of the 1960s with the likes of Jeanne Moreau and Jean-Luc Godard. This is what he rooted his entire identity as film critic in: he was there at this vibrant and exciting period of film history, getting drunk with actors on the sets of films that now count as classics.

Ronnie and I became very good friends in spite of our age difference partly because our tastes in art and film converged to a surprising degree. But Ronnie measured every contemporary film to his beloved classics, which is not a particularly helpful attitude if you spend half of your life on the festival circuit, where your job is to watch contemporary films. And Ronnie's attitude was not at all unusual among film critics: I have seen a lot of cultural pessimism and the glorification of the past in these circles. If these critics could get their kicks out of watching old films, but not new ones, then they may have been wasting their time on the festival circuit. But maybe they were not jaded at all. They just watched the wrong films. Or so I thought initially.

One night at the Chicago International Film Festival, after a particularly difficult jury decision and a lot of Amaretto, Ronnie confessed that he no longer got any pleasure out of seeing his old favourites. He said that sometimes he understood some interesting connections to other films or noticed some nuance that he could then write about in some review or article. But he no longer felt anything. Ronnie, understandably, was pretty cut up about this. And so was I.

Since then I've realized that this is a fairly widespread phenomenon among professional art critics and even art historians. Ernst Gombrich (1909–2001), probably the most widely known art historian of the 20th century, was in the exact same predicament. He could give a nuanced artistic and historical analysis of pretty much any painting he looked at, but the whole experience left him completely cold.

In fact, I was beginning to notice the signs of this in myself, with horror. I enjoyed watching films less and less, especially when I knew I had to write a review about them. And I have to admit that Ronnie was absolutely remarkable in that after seeing a film, he could just sit down and write a first-rate, sophisticated, and knowledgeable two-page review about it in ten minutes. So, I thought, maybe the price to pay for becoming a truly professional film critic is that we have to stop enjoying films? This possibility terrified me. Maybe this whole enjoyment-of-art thing is for amateurs only? True professionals don't waste time on that?

I don't think I have a good answer to these questions. But my stint as film critic did teach me to see what it was that Ronnie and his colleagues (and also, at least for some time, even myself) were doing: they had very clear and fixed expectations about what they were going to see when they sat down in the movie theatre.

Sweet, and not so sweet, expectations

Expectation is a good thing. Without having expectations about what is around us, we could do very little. And expectations also play a crucial role in our engagement with art: when we are listening to a song, even when we hear it for the first time, we have some expectations of how it will continue. And when it is a tune we know, this expectation can be quite strong (and easy to study experimentally). When we hear Ta-Ta-Ta at the beginning of Beethoven's *Fifth Symphony* (1808), we will strongly anticipate the closing Taaam of the Ta-Ta-Ta-Taaaam.

There is a lot of scientific research on how expectations can influence our experience—of music, of pain, of everything. And many of our expectations are fairly indeterminate: when we are listening to a musical piece we have never heard before, we will still have some expectations of how a tune will continue, but we don't know what exactly will happen. We can rule out that the violin glissando will continue with the sounds of a beeping alarm clock (unless it's a really avant-garde piece), but we can't predict with great certainty how exactly it will continue. Our expectations are malleable and dynamic: they change as we listen to the piece.

My suspicion is that the jaded critics' expectations are not so malleable and dynamic. Ronnie knew exactly what he could expect when the lights went off. No doubt, sometimes the film surprised him, but even if it did, it surprised him in a predictable manner: 'Aha, so the director chose a narrative twist that is reminiscent of Hitchcock, not of film noir!' The space of possibilities of what the film could do was already mapped out in his head at the very beginning. And the only degree of uncertainty was which of the already very clearly defined and understood rubrics the film would end up in.

Of course, the more you know about film, the more patterns of comparisons you will have, and it is very difficult to do anything in film that has not been done before. If you know the entirety of film history inside out, it is difficult to ignore these potential parallels, contrasts, and comparisons. But this can make your experience a mere classification job: the storyline was like *Indiana Jones* (1981), the composition like *Avatar* (2008), the acting like *Napoleon Dynamite* (2004). There's not much fun in watching films that way.

What is missing is some degree of openness and willingness to let yourself be genuinely surprised. Not just surprised about which carefully delineated film-historical pigeonhole the film ends up in. But surprised about what the film does to you.

The jaded film critic's attention is very much focused. Ronnie will focus on a couple of clearly defined features that he thinks will be relevant for his review. And he will ignore all the rest. And often rightly so, because the rest will probably be pretty predictable. But sometimes it will not be. And Ronnie will miss out on anything that happens outside the focus of his attention.

But if we watch a film with less clearly defined expectations (or should I say preconceptions?), we will not immediately discount everything that is outside the scope of those features we think are relevant. Everything can be relevant, even those things that the professional critic considers to be a waste of time.

André Breton (1896–1966), poet, artist, and the doyen of the Parisian Surrealist movement in the 1920s and 1930s, did not like cinema so much. He found it too predictable and too real—not quite up to his Surrealist standards. But he found a way to enjoy cinema by putting his opened-up left hand in front of his eyes, so he could not see the entire screen, only slices of it. And he claimed to have great experiences that way. Not something Ronnie would do, and, frankly, not something I would recommend to any budding film critic, but clearly a more enjoyable experience than Ronnie's.

By covering up half the screen, André Breton managed to get rid of his preconceptions of what would happen, and he could have a truly open experience of what was on the screen. Again, this is an extreme example, which would clearly not work for everyone. (And just imagine the sight of the entire audience covering up their eyes—not every film director's dream.) But that was André Breton's way of fighting the tendency to become jaded. What he did was to force his attention not to look for the usual stereotypical things one attends to. He forced his attention to be open and unconstrained by expectations. And there must be ways of doing this without covering your eyes.

Seeing afresh

About the same time that Breton was watching films through his fingers, the Italian painter Giorgio de Chirico (1888–1978) was painting hauntingly beautiful but also somewhat disconcerting paintings, with empty piazzas, arches, ancient sculptures, and trains in the distance. He had a particular talent for transforming everyday scenes into something out of this world. And he also had a lot to say about this:

> One clear autumnal afternoon I was sitting on a bench in the middle of the Piazza Santa Croce in Florence. It was of course not the first time I had seen this square. [...] The whole world, down to the marble of the buildings and the fountains, seemed to me to be convalescent. In the middle of the square rises a statue of Dante draped in a long cloak, holding his works clasped against his body, his laurel-crowned head bent thoughtfully earthward. The statue is in white marble, but time has given it a gray cast, very agreeable to

the eye. The autumn sun, warm and unloving, lit the statue and the
church façade. Then I had the strange impression that I was
looking at all these things for the first time.

What I find the most spot-on about this quote is the last sentence.
When we have strong experiences in front of an artwork or
landscapes, we often see it as if we were looking at it for the first
time. In fact, a good way of characterizing at least some forms of
aesthetic experience is that it feels as if it is the very first time we
are having this experience. Even if we have seen it many times
before, when it really touches us, it feels like it's the first time.
We've never *really* seen it before. But now we do.

This 'seeing it for the first time' line may sound like a corny cliché.
I think it's more than that. When you see something for the first
time, you have no established and routine way of looking at it—of
singling out those features that are relevant to you and of ignoring
the rest. You move your attention around, as any of its features
could be relevant. So when you see something for the first time,
your attention tends to be open-ended—you have no clear idea
what to focus on.

If you suddenly have to put out a fire in your friend's apartment
and you see an object (even an artwork) for the first time, you
probably won't move your attention around in search of rewarding
features. You'll just look out for one and only one thing: how it
can help you with putting out the fire. But if you are not in a hurry
to do anything in particular and you are interested in an object
you've never seen (and that's what happens in the museum,
typically), your attention tends to be open-ended. The feeling
that you're looking at something for the first time is an indication
that your attention is open-ended.

When you feel that you're looking at something for the first time,
this means that you've left behind any established and routine way
of looking at it. And this is the contrast I am interested in: routine

and habitual ways of looking at something and the 'as if for the first time' way of looking at it. This is what De Chirico was talking about: his routine and habitual way of relating to the world just stopped suddenly and he saw the world afresh.

Of course, there is nothing wrong with the routine and habitual. When driving to work, navigating a traffic jam, it is great to have the routine and habitual way of perceiving: in these occasions, you don't want to look at things afresh. Also, seeing afresh is difficult to maintain for more than just a couple of minutes. You can't be in this aesthetic trance 24/7.

Remember that song that you listened to over and over again as a teenager? Blew you away each time. Until, well, it just stopped blowing you away. It's as if you used it up; you got too used to it. Whenever that happened to me, I had a real feeling of loss.

The good thing is that at least sometimes this experience can come back. You stop listening to the song for a while and when, a couple of months (or years) later, you hear it again, it might blow you away even more strongly than ever before. And then, it *is* as if you were listening to it for the first time. The habits and routines melt away.

This was the key insight of De Chirico and his Parisian friends a hundred years ago: art can help us to overcome the habits and routines of our prosaic everyday perception. Habits grind you down. Even the most beautiful things will look paler and paler the more you look at them. But art can help you to let your habits go, and to look at something in a way you never have.

This 'seeing afresh' feeling obviously does not capture all we care about in aesthetic experiences. As we have seen, not all aesthetic experiences are characterized by the kind of open-ended attention that is at play when you see things as if you saw them for the first time. We clearly cherish listening to the same song hundreds

83

of times, watching the same movie until we know all the lines by heart, and so on. And we do enjoy the feeling of familiarity when we do so. Marcel Duchamp called art 'a habit-forming drug', no less. Aesthetic experiences come in different flavours. But some aesthetic experiences have a lot to do with seeing something as if we saw it for the first time.

The lingering effect

Here is another way in which the aesthetic colours our life. Aesthetic experiences can have a lingering effect. This is one odd and underexplored aspect of enjoying art: that it lingers. When you spend an entire day in the museum and you walk home afterwards, the drab bus stop may look to you like one of the pictures in the museum. And when you're leaving a good concert or movie, the ugly, grey, dirty streetscape can look positively beautiful.

Marcel Proust describes the same phenomenon. After seeing his favourite painter's work (he uses the fictional name of Elster to refer to him), he began paying attention to features in the prosaic dining room scene that he had never paid attention to before. He saw this scene that he had seen many, many times before very differently. Suddenly, he began to attend to

> the broken gestures of the knives still lying across one another, the
> swollen convexity of a discarded napkin upon which the sun would
> patch a scrap of yellow velvet, the half-empty glass which thus
> showed to greater advantage the noble sweep of its curved sides,
> and, in the heart of its translucent crystal, clear as frozen daylight,
> a dreg of wine, dusky but sparkling with reflected lights, the
> displacement of solid objects, the transmutation of liquids by the
> effect of light and shade, the shifting colour of the plums which
> passed from green to blue and from blue to golden yellow in the
> half-plundered dish, the chairs, like a group of old ladies, that came
> twice daily to take their places round the white cloth spread on the

table as on an altar at which were celebrated the rites of the palate, where in the hollows of oyster-shells a few drops of lustral water had gathered as in tiny holy water stoups of stone…

As he says, 'I tried to find beauty there where I had never imagined before that it could exist, in the most ordinary things, in the profundities of "still life".'

One of the advantages of emphasizing the importance of attention in aesthetic engagement is that it can explain this puzzling phenomenon. Art changes the way you attend. And this attentional state of mind doesn't stop just like that. It lingers on.

Aesthetic experiences can make us ditch our preconceived way of making sense of what we see. When we're done with the art, our attentional freedom takes some time to change back. We keep on approaching whatever we see with open-ended attention. And this can lead to seeing the dirty sidewalk in front of the cinema as a work of art.

Ad Reinhardt (1913–67), the American abstract painter, says that 'looking isn't so simple as it looks. Art teaches people how to see.' And this is one important perk we get from enjoying art: it can make you recover the uncomplicated pleasure of seeing—regardless of what it is that you are seeing. It *can* make you see things as if you were looking at them for the very first time.

Chapter 7
Global aesthetics

Think back to your last visit to a major art museum. Can you recall how many of the 'must see' artworks in the museum were made in Europe or the US? Probably the vast majority of them. But artworks have been made in all parts of the world, not only in Europe and the US. These artworks are not easy to spot in most art museums. If they are there at all, they tend to be tucked away in some distant wing.

Willem de Kooning (1904–97), the abstract expressionist painter, compared the dominant contemporary vision of art history to a railway track: 'There is a train track in the history of art that goes back to Mesopotamia. It skips the whole Orient, the Mayas, and American Indians. Duchamp is on it. Cézanne is on it. Picasso and the Cubists are on it; Giacometti, Mondrian, and so many, many more—whole civilizations.'

Luckily, few art historians subscribe to this single railway track vision of art history these days. But this way of thinking about art still dominates everyday conceptions of art and also curatorial work in most museums. If we want to stop privileging European art over any other kind of art, we need to change not just the imbalance between 'Western' and non-'Western' art, but also the imbalance between 'Western' and non-'Western' aesthetics. We need a global aesthetics.

The geography of vision

How does your aesthetic experience (your experience of artworks, landscape, etc.) depend on what culture you grew up in? This is the starting question of global aesthetics. And the answer is straightforward: we can't just assume that artefacts are perceived everywhere and in every historical era the way they are perceived here and now. (I will talk about artefacts from now on because I want to stay away from the question about what does and what does not count as 'art' in which cultures.)

This claim goes against a traditional view in aesthetics, according to which aesthetics as a discipline is about universals: it examines ways of engaging with artworks and other aesthetic objects that are independent of our cultural background. In fact, art historians often accuse aestheticians of this kind of cultural universalism. And this universalism of aesthetics is even more heavily emphasized by the recently fashionable neuroscientifically tainted aesthetic research, which often aims to find the neural correlates of various forms of aesthetic appreciation in a way that does not depend on the cultural background of the subjects.

In fact, it's the other way around. If we take the empirical sciences of the mind seriously, what they actually teach us is to abandon cultural universalism altogether. The reason for this is the well-documented abundance of top–down influences on perception. Thousands of studies in psychology and neuroscience demonstrate that what we know and believe influences even the earliest stages of visual and auditory processing. And given that we know and believe different things depending on what culture and what time period we grew up in, our perception will also be different depending on what culture and what time period we grew up in.

The question is how these top–down influences on perception work and what processes mediate them. I will talk about two such mediating mechanisms, attention and mental imagery. Both attention and mental imagery depend heavily on our higher order mental states, such as beliefs and knowledge. And both attention and mental imagery influence our perception and our aesthetic engagement.

To put it differently, there are cross-cultural variations in attention and mental imagery. And given the importance of attention and mental imagery in our aesthetic engagement, this guarantees that there will be cross-cultural variations in our aesthetic engagement. Knowing what we know about how the mind works, universalism is not an option. We can't assume that our engagement is the same as the engagement intended and practised by the local producers and users of the artefact.

What we are attending to and how we do so very much depend on our background beliefs, knowledge, and perceptual skills, all of which are culturally specific. So our patterns of attention are also culturally specific. But given that our experience of artefacts depends heavily on what we are attending to, this means that there is significant cross-cultural variation in our experience of artefacts.

Here is an example: look at the tepatu (breastplate) from the Solomon Islands shown in Figure 5. You probably see an abstract pattern of intersecting lines. Now I tell you that the inverted V shape at the lower end of the tepatu is likely to represent the tail of the frigate bird, and the shapes just above them are its wings. The frigate bird indicates the presence of schools of bonito, a fish crucial in the diet of inhabitants of Santa Cruz Islands, where this tepatu is from. The shapes further up are thought to represent dolphins or fish, maybe even the bonito that frigate birds signal.

You are likely to attend to different features of this tepatu before and after reading the previous paragraph. You pay more attention to parts of it that you ignored before (e.g. the little bumps which

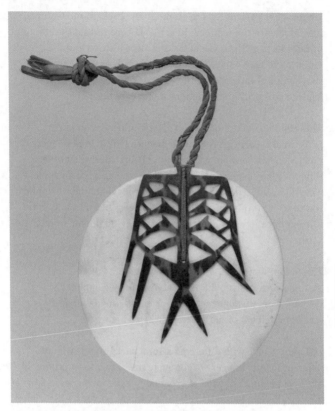

5. **Tepatu (or tema or tambe), Solomon Islands, late 19th century (Oceania), Metropolitan Museum of Art.**

may indicate the backs of dolphins). And, as a result, your experience is very different. Change in (very culturally specific) attention leads to change in your experience of the artefact.

And it is not just what we attend to that differs across cultures, but also the way we attend. People who grew up in East Asia tend to respond differently from Europeans to simple visual displays, like an aquarium. Europeans tend to attend to the moving fish, whereas East Asians tend to attend to the background features, like bubbles or the seaweed. In general, it seems that the attention of Europeans in these visual tasks is more focused and the attention of East Asians is more distributed. Again, there are cross-cultural variations in the exercise of attention, which then leads to cross-cultural variations in our experience.

The second mediator of the top–down influences on our perceptual experience is mental imagery. Our mental imagery very much depends on what we know and believe and what other things we have perceived before. When you visualize an apple, the way this visualized apple looks depends on what kinds of apples you've seen in your life. And mental imagery plays an important role in our experience of artworks (a recurring theme in Japanese aesthetics).

The Indonesian artist, Jompet Kuswidananto (1976–), for example, creates installations that need to be completed with the help of mental imagery. The spectator's mental imagery is a crucial ingredient of the experience here (Figure 6).

Different people with different cultural backgrounds will use different mental imagery to complete this artwork—presumably most people (not all) will have mental imagery of horses looking at this installation, but in those cultures where horses are associated with warfare, for example, this mental imagery (especially of the rider) will be very different and it will carry very different emotional charge. And this means that different people with different cultural background will have very different experiences of the very same artwork.

The Kuswidananto installation has unusually direct and explicit appeal on our mental imagery, but mental imagery is involved in almost all experiences of artworks. This is especially clear in almost all non-'Western' aesthetic traditions, where aesthetic experience is very explicitly taken to be a multimodal experience

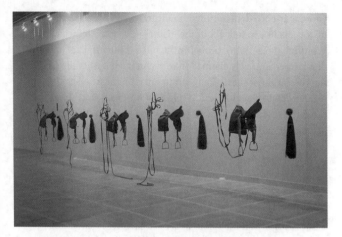

6. Jompet Kuswidananto, *Cortège of the Third Realm*, 2012 (Indonesia).

that talks to all our sense modalities, not just to vision, but also hearing, smelling, tasting, and touching (the often quite extreme visuo-centrism of aesthetics seems to be a 'Western' thing).

This is most explicitly articulated in the Rasa tradition, where, as we have seen, Rasa literally means the savouring of the emotional flavour of experience. And flavour here is not a mere metaphor. Even those Rasa experiences that are triggered by only one sense modality (say, hearing, in the case of music) are supposed to exercise all of our other sense modalities (seeing, smelling, touching, tasting). In other words, they are supposed to evoke multimodal mental imagery.

And the Rasa is not an isolated example. A key concept in Japanese aesthetics is that of 'hidden beauty' or Yugen, the appreciation of which involves something akin to mental imagery (of the hidden and incomplete aspects). And the 11th-century Islamic philosopher Avicenna also heavily emphasized the importance of imagery in our experience of beauty.

Our experience depends on our cultural background. Art historians like to talk about the history of vision. Heinrich Wölfflin (1864–1945), probably the most influential art historian of all time, famously claimed that 'vision itself has its history, and the revelation of these visual strata must be regarded as the primary task of art history'. While a lot has been said about this provocative statement, there is one sense in which this claim is just empirically true: given that attention and mental imagery have a history, vision, which is influenced by these, also has a history.

If vision has a history in this sense, then vision also has a geography. And the same is true of perception in general. Given that attention and mental imagery are exercised depending on what culture we have grown up in, perception, which is influenced by these, also depends on our cultural background. Global aesthetics is about the geography of vision.

A global vocabulary

We can't use our own experience of an artefact to make assumptions about how this artefact is experienced in different cultures. But then how are we supposed to find out about how it is experienced and used in different cultures (especially if nobody is left from these cultures to talk to)?

We know a lot about some centres of artefact production. We know much less about others. This introduces a significant asymmetry into thinking about global aesthetics. We have a fair amount of information about how paintings were made and how people looked at them in 15th-century Italy and we know almost nothing about this in 15th-century Central America. This epistemic asymmetry is a result of coincidental factors like where records survived and where they did not. This should not lead us to think that artefacts in those parts of the world that we know more about are somehow 'better' or more worthy of study.

But if we can't extrapolate our 'Western' experience to other cultures and if we have very little information about how artefacts were experienced in most parts of the world, then this leads to a sceptical conclusion—we just have no way of knowing how other cultures experience artefacts because of the radical differences of the experience of artefacts in different cultures. If we want to avoid this sceptical conclusion, we need to find a way of understanding at least some aspects of artefacts without knowing much about the culture that produced them.

Global aesthetics must be able to have a conceptual framework that can talk about any artefact, no matter where and when it was made. This amounts to identifying features that every artefact needs to have and that are aesthetically relevant.

Some trivial examples of features that every artefact needs to have include material composition and size. Every artefact is made of something and every artefact is either this or that big. There are even more trivial features such as whether or not the artefact depicts an apple. It either does or it doesn't—there are no other options. The problem with these examples is that while in some cultures size and material composition may be aesthetically relevant, in many cultures, they are not. We need to find some feature-space that is more aesthetically relevant.

I want to use pictures as a case study. The experience of pictures can often be an aesthetic experience, and this is true not just in our 'Western' culture. Pictures are not necessarily artworks—for example, airplane safety charts about how to leave the plane in case of a water landing are not artworks by any account. Lots of things count as pictures: not just oil on canvas or tempera on wood, but also tattoos on one's skin, scratches on a piece of tree bark, or selfies on your phone. Pictures are a diverse bunch.

Nonetheless, every picture has pictorial organization: every picture organizes the pictorial elements in a non-random manner. And pictorial organization is aesthetically significant in all cultures. One of the key concepts of Yoruba aesthetics (the aesthetic tradition of the people of South-West Nigeria) is that of 'ifarahon', which is often translated as visibility—as the requirement that all parts of the person are clearly formed and visible. While this concept initially applied to sculptures, it has also become the most important virtue photographers should aim for (where it would, for example, imply that both of the sitter's eyes should be visible).

In the most detailed early work of Chinese aesthetics of painting, the 6th-century Chinese painter and critic Xie He outlined the six laws of painting. The fifth one is about placing and arranging on the surface the pictorial elements in space and depth (which became a central topic in all Chinese treatises on paintings from then on). The third Khanda of *Vishnudharmottara Purana*, the extremely detailed encyclopedic Hindu text on painting, written about the same time, is also full of references to pictorial organization—who should be behind or next to or in front of whom. And pictorial organization has been a central topic of Japanese aesthetics as well.

The question all these works ask is how pictures are organized. On a very abstract level, there are two different and distinctive modes of pictorial organization, which I call 'surface organization' and 'scene organization'. Every picture, regardless of where and when it was made, falls somewhere on the spectrum between surface organization and scene organization.

Surface organization aims to draw attention to how the two-dimensional outline shapes of the depicted objects are placed within the two-dimensional frame. Scene organization, in contrast, aims to draw attention to how the three-dimensional depicted objects are placed in the depicted space. There is a trade-off between the two and most pictures are trying to combine them. But one—either scene or surface organization—tends to win out when the two organizational principles are in conflict.

Pictorial organization is aesthetically relevant and all picture makers need to choose how to organize their pictures. And, crucially, this is not a 'West'-centric distinction—it is a design problem for pictures in any culture. Thus, the spectrum between scene organization and surface organization could be taken to be a starting point of a very general (but not 'West'-centric) conceptual framework for describing any pictures, regardless of where they were made.

The distinction between scene organization and surface organization is somewhat abstract. So it would be helpful to substantiate this distinction with the help of simpler features that are easier to spot. I will focus on two such features: occlusion and empty surface.

In everyday perception, we get a lot of occlusion: we see some objects behind or in front of other objects. The question is whether occlusion shows up in pictures. Surface organization implies that the picture maker pays attention to whether there is occlusion or not: occlusion in a picture is a feature of how two-dimensional outline shapes of the depicted objects are related to each other on the two-dimensional surface. Some pictures go out of their way to avoid occlusion. Some others pile on occlusions. Both are good indications of surface organization. And we can place all pictures on a spectrum between extreme lack of occlusion and extreme seeking out of occlusion. Figures 7 and 8 are two examples that are close to the two end points.

Pictures from some cultures will cluster around specific points of this occlusion spectrum. The Scythian pictures of Pazyryk, for example, tend to avoid occlusion at almost all costs. In Hanegawa

7. **Scythian wall-hanging, 5th century** BCE, **Pazyryk, Altai** (**Siberia**).

Toei's image, almost everything seems to be deliberately occluded. Both of these types of pictures would count as having surface organization.

Pictures of some other cultures (for example, Plane Native American carvings or Dutch still life paintings from the 17th century), in contrast, are not particularly bothered by the presence or lack of occlusion—this is an indication of scene organization: if a picture is organized in terms of the three-dimensional scene it depicts, then neither occlusion nor the lack of occlusion will be particularly important.

The second feature that every picture has is the presence or absence of empty surface. In everyday perception, some of our visual field is often empty in the sense that there are no perceptually interesting elements there—only the sky, the ground,

8. Hanegawa Toei, *Procession of Korean Mission in Edo*, c.1748 (Japan).

an empty wall. Some pictures deliberately try to avoid empty surface: they try to put pictorially interesting elements on every square inch of the surface. Others deliberately seek out empty surfaces. Some examples are found in Figures 9 and 10.

Again, paying attention to whether some part of the surface is empty or not is very much an indicator of surface organization. Scene organization is neutral about whether some parts of the surface remain unfilled. As in the case of occlusion, pictures with surface organization will cluster around some specific points of the empty surface spectrum (pictures from different cultures around different points). Pictures with scene organization, in contrast, are scattered around much of this spectrum.

We get a coordinate system on the basis of these two features: occlusion and empty surface. And we can add other features like frame or symmetry. Some pictures respect or even emphasize their

9. Alexander Apóstol, Residente Pulido, 2001 (the photographer digitally removed many of the details (windows, doors) from the building) (Venezuela).

frame, others deliberately try to pretend that the frame is not there. And as the frame is very much a two-dimensional surface feature, paying attention to it (either by emphasizing it or by de-emphasizing it) is a sign of surface organization. Symmetry is another surface feature: going out of your way to get symmetrical

10. **Mural in Wat Pho, 19th century, Bangkok School (Thailand).**

compositions or going out of your way to get asymmetrical compositions would then be an indication of surface organization. If symmetry is not a big deal (or if the frame is not a big deal), that would be a sign of scene organization.

This gives rise to a multi-dimensional feature space where we can place every picture, regardless of how much we know about the culture that produced it. This is obviously not the end of our understanding of pictures from different cultures: there are so many other aspects of pictures that are culturally specific that this formal analysis will not be able to provide. But it is a solid starting point for any further, more culturally specific enquiry.

This culture-neutral multi-dimensional feature-space can help us to make some progress in understanding pictures of cultures we otherwise know very little about. If all pictures produced in a specific culture painstakingly avoid occlusion, for example, this gives us an important data point to try to find out why they do so. This formal analysis will not give us answers (or it may give us very partial answers), but it can make the questions we ask more focused.

Here is an example. If you knew nothing about medieval European culture and you saw many images like Domenico Veneziano's small painting we encountered in Chapter 5 (Figure 4), you would have no idea who the two figures in these images are. One of them is a woman, the other one has wings. But if you see enough images of this woman plus winged human pattern, you would notice that the two figures tend to be placed far away from each other. Not only do they not occlude one another, but they are placed on the canvas in such a way that they could not possibly occlude one another. You do not know that these are images of the Annunciation, the meeting between a human and an angel who inhabit very different spiritual realms, and, as a result, they could not (or should not) really be depicted in the same space. You would only know this if you knew at least something about medieval European religion and culture. But even if you had no information about medieval European culture whatsoever, just by noticing the oddities of the spatial relation between these two figures, you would at least be in the position to identify this culturally specific oddity. In order to understand why this is a design problem in medieval Annunciations, you would need to know something about the local (medieval European) culture. But you can notice this design problem without any culture-specific information.

Global aesthetics is based on the mutually strengthening interactions between culturally specific information and very general formal features that every artefact of a certain kind shares. These two seemingly opposite tendencies can and should help each other: the more we find out about some recurring formal feature of the artefacts in a certain culture (for example, whether they deliberately avoid occlusion), the better position we are in to look for some culturally specific information about why they do so.

Even more lost in the museum

I started the book with an experience all of us have when facing works of art or other objects of aesthetic importance—we sometimes just find it difficult to get into the swing of having an aesthetic experience no matter how hard we try. You have had strong and rewarding aesthetic experiences in front of this artwork. But just now it's not happening.

Here is a more specific question that you probably ask yourself in the museum even more often: what should I look for when I am encountering artefacts from different cultures? Take a West African sculpture from Benin (Figure 11). It is highly likely that these sculptures were not meant to be engaged with aesthetically (regardless of how broadly we interpret what counts as aesthetic). What do you do when you enter a room in a museum full of 16th-century Beninese sculptures like this? What kind of experience do you try to have?

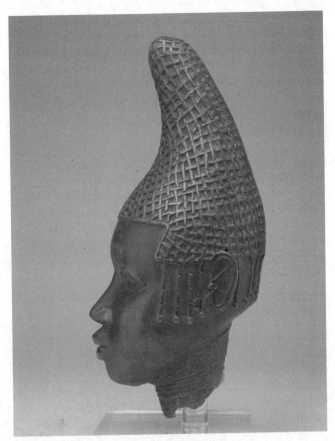

11. *Head of the Queen Mother*, 16th-century (Benin).

My guess is that you are trying to make sense of these objects by relating them to artworks you know. In the case of the West African sculpture, this reference frame is, for many of us, likely to be European modernist sculpture (which, not at all incidentally, was heavily influenced by West African wood carvings). We might be drawn to some sculptures from Benin because they remind us

12. **Constantin Brâncuşi, *Maiastra* (Guggenheim Museum).**

of the modernist sculpture of, say, Constantin Brâncuşi (1876–1957) (Figure 12). And we could take a fair amount of aesthetic pleasure and maybe even aesthetic experience out of this.

I made a sociological claim: I described how we do in fact tend to engage with objects of this kind. But there is a further question: is it wrong if we engage with artefacts in this way? These objects were clearly not meant to be experienced like a Brâncuşi.

A similar question is this: What are we looking for when we encounter artefacts from a different time period? Going to a museum very often implies that you will encounter artefacts from a different time period. Same for listening to music or reading literature. What do we do when we do this?

Again, my sociological claim is that we are trying to experience these works in a way that we can relate to: in ways we are familiar with from our engagement with works from our present. When we look at the Domenico Veneziano painting in Chapter 5, we are trying to look at it in a way that was shaped by our encounter with very different kinds of (say, 20th-century) paintings. The question remains: is it wrong if we do this?

In the light of the culture-specificity of our aesthetic experience, the questions about what's wrong and what's right when it comes to engaging with artworks do not even arise. They do not arise because whether or not it's wrong to engage with Beninese sculpture and early Italian painting as if they were modernist artworks, we don't really have an alternative. The best we can do is to evaluate these artworks from the distance of our own culture.

As we have seen, aesthetic experience is influenced in a top–down manner by one's cultural background. The Beninese sculptor and the people who were the intended audience of the sculptures had very different top–down influences on their aesthetic engagements from the ones I have. This makes it very unlikely that we're engaging in the same way the original producers and users of the artefact did.

But couldn't we at least try to bridge this gap? We could try. And, in some sense, we should. Needless to say, it can be immensely rewarding to learn about other cultures and their artefacts. But there is a systematic reason why full cultural immersion is close to impossible and it is a psychological phenomenon we know very well by now: the mere exposure effect (the repeated exposure to the concept of mere exposure effect throughout this book should really make any reader be positively disposed to it). Because of the mere exposure effect, our value judgements depend on what works we've encountered. Our imprinted aesthetic preferences (dictated by what we have encountered in early formative years) are very, very difficult to shake.

We can spend decades exploring a different culture *in situ*. In fact, this is what many global art historians do. If they research, say, Indonesian art, then they move to Indonesia for many years, even decades, exposing themselves to the cultural milieu, and the stimuli in that milieu that might be very different from the stimuli they are used to. And this can, at least partially, reverse the mere exposure effect. But life is short: even if you get fully immersed in, say, Indonesian culture, you would still be completely lost at an exhibition of Maya art.

Aesthetic humility again

Michael Baxandall (1933–2008), the British art historian and critic, made a distinction between the participants and the observers of a culture. As he says, 'the participant understands and knows [her] culture with an immediacy and spontaneity the observer does not share. [She] can act within the culture's standards and norms without rational self-consciousness.'

My point is that it is very difficult, in fact, close to impossible to fully become participants in a different culture. The default is that we will always remain observers, in spite of all our efforts. Just because we have read a couple of books about Oceanian art, we do not suddenly become participants. And the reason for this is mainly empirical: the top–down influences on perception and the mere exposure effect.

What to do about this? It is still a good idea to read up on distant cultures and forms of art production as it can be immensely rewarding. And global aesthetics should go at least some distance towards understanding how people in other cultures might have seen the world around them. By reading up on distant cultures we can bring them a little bit closer and this can open up thus far unknown aesthetic experiences. But nobody should be deluded into thinking that by doing so we can become participants rather than mere distant observers.

And this gives us even more reason to exercise aesthetic humility. We should always be aware of the cultural perspective that we occupy and treat our aesthetic evaluations with humility: as an evaluation made from a very specific cultural perspective. It is easy to be arrogant about aesthetics—maybe precisely because it matters so much to us personally. But this is all the more reason to be extra careful with our aesthetic evaluations. If there is one take-home message of this book, it is that we all need more aesthetic humility.

References

Chapter 1: Lost in the museum

The Gombrowicz quote is from his *Diaries* (New Haven: Yale University Press, 2012), p. 39.

The Léger story is in his The Machine Aesthetic. *Bulletin de l'effort moderne* (Paris, 1924).

The Newman quote is from John P. O'Neill (ed.), *Barnett Newman: Selected Writings and Interviews* (New York: Alfred A. Knopf, 1990), p. 25.

The 'influential strand in Western aesthetics' goes back to Immanuel Kant's *Critique of Judgement*.

On the importance of the aesthetics of everyday scenes, see Sherri Irvin, The Pervasiveness of the Aesthetic in Ordinary Experience. *British Journal of Aesthetics* 48 (2008): 29–44; Bence Nanay, Aesthetic Experience of Artworks and Everyday Scenes. *The Monist* 101 (2018): 71–82; Yuriko Saito, *Everyday Aesthetics* (Oxford: Oxford University Press, 2007).

Chapter 2: Sex, drugs, and rock 'n' roll

A good exposition of the 'sex, drugs, and rock 'n' roll' problem is in Jerrold Levinson's *The Pleasures of Aesthetics* (Ithaca, NY: Cornell University Press, 1996).

What I call the 'beauty-salon approach' can be found in almost all 'Western' texts on beauty from Plato to Mary Mothersill: see Mary Mothersill, *Beauty Restored* (Oxford: Clarendon Press, 1984).

The Oscar Wilde quote is from his 1879 lecture to art students. In his *Essays and Lectures* (London: Methuen, 1911), p. 111.

A very democratic account of beauty, and one that is broadly congruous
with my approach is in Dominic Lopes's *Being for Beauty* (Oxford:
Oxford University Press, 2018).

The Léger quote is from: The Machine Aesthetic: The Manufactured
Object, the Artisan and the Artist. *Bulletin de l'effort moderne*
(Paris, 1924).

For Kant's concept of disinterested pleasure, see Immanuel Kant,
Critique of Judgement, trans. W. S. Pluhar (Indianapolis: Hackett,
1987, originally 1790).

A good summary of the distinction between restoration pleasure and
tonic pleasure is in Michael Kubovy, On the Pleasures of the Mind.
In: D. Kahneman, E. Diener, and N. Schwartz (eds), *Well-Being:
Foundations of Hedonic Psychology* (New York: Russell Sage
Foundation, 1999), pp. 134–49.

The best worked-out account of aesthetic pleasure as sustaining
pleasure is Mohan Matthen's theory. See his The Pleasure of Art.
Australasian Philosophical Review 1 (2017): 6–28. What I call
'relief pleasure', Matthen calls 'r-pleasure' (and Kubovy 'restoration
pleasure'); what I call 'sustaining pleasure', Matthen calls 'f-pleasure'
(and Kubovy 'tonic pleasure').

Laura Mulvey's article was published in *Screen* 16/3 (1975): 6–18.

The Iris Murdoch quote is from her Existentialist Hero, *The Listener*
23 (March 1950), p. 52.

The Kubler quote is from George Kubler, *The Shape of Time* (New
Haven: Yale University Press, 1962), p. 80.

On wonder as an aesthetic emotion, see Jesse Prinz, *Works of Wonder*
(New York: Oxford University Press, forthcoming).

On being moved as an aesthetic emotion, see Florian Cova and Julien
Deonna, Being Moved. *Philosophical Studies* 169 (2014): 447–66
(although they never make the claim that this is a universal feature
of all aesthetic engagement).

On contemplation of formal features as an aesthetic emotion, see Clive
Bell, *Art* (London: Chatto and Windus, 1914).

For an argument that all actions are emotional actions, see Bence
Nanay, All Actions are Emotional Actions. *Emotion Review*
9 (2017): 350–2.

The quote by Fernando Pessoa is from his *The Book of Disquiet*
(London: Serpent's Tail, 1991), p. 27 (29 [87]).

The Sontag quote is in her essay On Style (1965), in her *Against
Interpretation* (New York: Farrar Straus Giroux, 1986), p. 27.

A good example of the 'valuing for its own sake' approach is chapter 3
    of Robert Stecker's *Aesthetics and Philosophy of Art* (Lanham, Md:
    Rowman and Littlefield, 2005).

For more on the trophy–process balance, see <https://www.
    psychologytoday.com/intl/blog/psychology-tomorrow/201812/
    the-trophy-process-balance>.

The Huxley book is *The Doors of Perception* (London: Chatto and
    Windus, 1954).

The Proust quote is from his *Sodom and Gomorrah*, chapter II,
    paragraph 25 (p. 138 in the Moncrieff translation).

Chapter 3: Experience and attention

For some more visual examples of the difference attention
    can make in your aesthetic and non-aesthetic experiences,
    see <https://aestheticsforbirds.com/2014/06/16/
    paying-aesthetic-attention-bence-nanay/>.

The Gorilla experiment: D. J. Simmons and C. F. Chabris, Gorillas in
    our Midst: Sustained Inattentional Blindness for Dynamic Events.
    Perception 28 (1999): 1059–74. There are some dissenting voices
    that construe the phenomenon not as inattentional blindness, but
    as inattentional amnesia (we see the gorilla but then immediately
    forget that we have seen it). See J. M. Wolfe, Inattentional
    Amnesia. In: V. Coltheart (ed.), *Fleeting Memories. Cognition of
    Brief Visual Stimuli* (Cambridge, Mass.: MIT Press, 1999).

A good summary of the psychological research on focused versus
    distributed attention is in Arien Mack, Is the Visual World a Grand
    Illusion? *Journal of Consciousness Studies* 9 (2002): 102–10.

For a more detailed account of focused versus distributed attention,
    see Bence Nanay, *Aesthetics as Philosophy of Perception* (Oxford:
    Oxford University Press, 2016).

The Danièle Huillet line is from a 2005 interview with Tag Gallagher,
    Senses of Cinema, 2005, Issue 37.

The Maria Abramovic quote is from a 2012 interview with Ross
    Simonini, *Globe and Mail* 20 February 2012.

The quote by Fernando Pessoa is from his *The Book of Disquiet*
    (London: Serpent's Tail, 1991), p. 77 (76 [389]).

On the role of experience in Sanskrit aesthetics and Rasa theory in
    general, see Sheldon Pollock (ed.), *A Rasa Reader* (New York:
    Columbia University Press, 2016).

A good summary of the transparency of perception is in Laura Gow's
The Limitations of Perceptual Transparency. *Philosophical
Quarterly* 66 (2016): 723–44.

Chapter 4: Aesthetics and the self

The findings about the importance of aesthetic preferences for the self
started with the publication of Nina Strohminger and Shaun
Nichols, The Essential Moral Self. *Cognition* 131 (2014): 159–71,
and various responses to this paper. See esp. J. Fingerhut,
J. Gomez-Lavin, C. Winklmayr, and J. J. Prinz, The Aesthetic Self.
In: *Frontiers in Psychology* (forthcoming).

On the findings about the constant changes in our aesthetic
preferences, see Cambeon Pugach, Helmut Leder, and
Daniel J. Graham, How Stable are Human Aesthetic Preferences
across the Lifespan. *Frontiers in Human Neuroscience* 11 (2017):
289. doi: 10.3389/fnhum.2017.00289.

The phenomenon that we think we don't change but we do even has a
fancy label, 'The End of History Illusion'. See <https://www.ted.
com/talks/bence_nanay_the_end_of_history_illusion>.

The mere exposure effect experiment with the impressionist paintings
is reported in James E. Cutting, The Mere Exposure Effect and
Aesthetic Preference. In: P. Locher et al. (eds), *New Directions in
Aesthetics, Creativity and the Psychology of Art* (New York:
Baywood, 2007), pp. 33–46. See also Bence Nanay, Perceptual
Learning, the Mere Exposure Effect and Aesthetic Antirealism.
Leonardo 50 (2017): 58–63.

For a good illustration of how judgement-centred aesthetics is, see
Malcolm Budd, Aesthetic Judgements, Aesthetic Principles and
Aesthetic Properties. *European Journal of Philosophy* 7/3 (1999):
295–311.

A good exposition of how aesthetics should not bypass talking about
the pleasure we take in aesthetic phenomena is Jerrold Levinson's
Pleasure and the Value of Works of Art, in his *The Pleasures of
Aesthetics* (Ithaca, NY: Cornell University Press, 1996).

The Susan Sontag quote is from her essay On Style (originally
published in 1965), reprinted in her *Against Interpretation* (New
York: Farrar Straus Giroux, 1986), p. 21.

Hume's essay is Of the Standard of Taste (1757), in *Essays: Moral,
Political and Literary*, ed. Eugene Miller (Indianapolis: Liberty,
1985). A very thorough analysis of Hume's argument is in Jerrold

Levinson's Hume's Standard of Taste: The Real Problem. *Journal of Aesthetics and Art Criticism* 60/3 (2002): 227–38.

On the role of experience in Islamic aesthetics, see Valerie Gonzalez, *Beauty and Islam: Aesthetics in Islamic Art and Architecture* (London: I. B. Tauris, 2001). See also J. N. Erzen, Islamic Aesthetics: An Alternative Way to Knowledge. *Journal of Aesthetics and Art Criticism* 65/1 (2007): 69–75.

On the concept of 'tabritu' in Assyro-Babylonian aesthetics, see Irene J. Winter, The Eyes Have lt: Votive Statuary, Gilgamesh's Axe, and Cathected Viewing in the Ancient Near East. In: Robert S. Nelson (ed.), *Visuality Before and Beyond the Renaissance: Seeing as Others Saw* (Cambridge: Cambridge University Press, 2000), pp. 22–44.

Chapter 5: Aesthetics and the other

Here is what Pauline Kael said: 'I regard criticism as an art, and if in this country and in this age, it is practised with honesty, it is no more remunerative than the work of an avant-garde film artist.' See her *I Lost It at the Movies: The Essential Kael Collection '54–'65* (London: Marion Boyars, 2002), p. 234.

The Eagleton quote is in his *The Function of Criticism* (London: Verso, 1984), p. 7.

The Malraux line is from André Malraux, *Museum without Walls* (New York: Doubleday, 1967), p. 236.

Chapter 6: Aesthetics and life

The Berenice Abbott quote is from Julia Van Haaften, *Berenice Abbott: A Life in Photography* (New York: W. W. Norton, 2018).

The Robert Musil quip is in his novel *The Man without Qualities*, trans. Eithne Wilkins and Ernst Kaiser (London: Picador, 1979) (1930/2). Volume II, p. 336.

The Camus quote is in his posthumously published *A Happy Death* (New York: Penguin, 2002).

A vivid expression of Oscar Wilde's line on being the spectator of one's own life is in his novel *The Picture of Dorian Grey* (New York: Barnes and Noble, 1995), p. 121.

Arthur Schopenhauer was another influential proponent of the idea of aesthetic contemplation. See esp. his *The World as Will and Representation* (Cambridge: Cambridge University Press, 2011).

The Sontag quote is in her essay On Style (1965), in her *Against Interpretation* (New York: Farrar Straus Giroux, 1986), p. 27.

The André Gide quote is from his *Diary*, 25 July 1934.

The Stendhal quote is in chapter 23 of his novel *Charterhouse of Parma*.

The quote by Giorgio de Chirico is from his 'Meditations of a Painter, 1912'. In Herschel B. Chipp (ed.), *Theories of Modern Art* (Berkeley: University of California Press, 1968), pp. 397–8.

The general idea of art working against our habits is often associated with Russian formalism. See e.g. Victor Shklovsky, 'Art as Technique' (1917). In *Russian Formalist Criticism: Four Essays*, ed. Lee T. Lemon and Marion J. Reis (Lincoln, Nebr.: University of Nebraska Press, 1965). See also Bence Nanay, Defamiliarization and the Unprompted (not Innocent) Eye. *Nonsite* 24 (2018): 1–17.

The Duchamp quote is from Calvin Tomkins, *The Afternoon Interviews* (Brooklyn: Badlands, 2013), p. 55.

The long Proust quote is from *Within a Budding Grove*, trans. C. K. Scott Moncrieff (New York: Vintage, 1970), p. 325.

The Ad Reinhardt quote is from his 'How to Look at Things through a Wine-glass'. *PM*, 7 July 1946.

Chapter 7: Global aesthetics

The De Kooning train-track analogy is from his 'The Renaissance and Order'. *Trans/formation* 1 (1951): 86–7.

For a summary of the literature on top–down influences on perception, see Christoph Teufel and Bence Nanay, How to (and how not to) Think about Top-down Influences on Perception. *Consciousness and Cognition* 47 (2017): 17–25.

For the cross-cultural findings about what we attend to when we are looking at an aquarium, see Takahiko Masuda and Richard E. Nisbett, Attending Holistically versus Analytically: Comparing the Context Sensitivity of Japanese and Americans. *Journal of Personality and Social Psychology* 81 (2001): 922–34.

On mental imagery and the important role it plays in aesthetics, see Bence Nanay, *Seeing Things You Don't See* (Oxford: Oxford University Press, forthcoming).

On the multimodality of our aesthetic experiences in the Rasa tradition, see K. M. Higgins, An Alchemy of Emotion: Rasa and Aesthetic Breakthroughs. *Journal of Aesthetics and Art Criticism*

65/1 (2007): 43–54; see also Bence Nanay, The Multimodal
Experience of Art. *British Journal of Aesthetics* 52 (2012): 353–63.

On 'hidden beauty' or Yugen, see T. Izutsu, and T. Izutsu, *The Theory
of Beauty in the Classical Aesthetics of Japan* (The Hague:
Martinus Nijhoff, 1981). See also Y. Saiko, The Japanese Aesthetics
of Imperfection and Insufficiency. *Journal of Aesthetics and Art
Criticism* 55/4 (1997): 377–85.

On Avicenna and imagery, see Valerie Gonzales, *Beauty and Islam*
(London: I. B. Tauris Publishers, 2001), esp. pp. 16–18.

The Wölfflin quote is from his 1915 *Principles of Art History* (New
York: Dover, 1932), p. 11.

More on the history of vision debate in Bence Nanay, The History of
Vision. *Journal of Aesthetics and Art Criticism* 73 (2015): 259–71.

On just how much we know about how paintings were looked at in
15th-century Italy, see Michael Baxandall, *Painting and Experience
in Fifteenth Century Italy* (Oxford: Oxford University Press, 1972).

On 'ifarahon' and Yoruba aesthetics in general, see
Stephen F. Sprague: Yoruba photography. *African Art* 12 (1978):
52–107.

On Xie He's aesthetics of painting, see H. Saussy, *The Problem of a
Chinese Aesthetic* (Stanford, Calif.: Stanford University Press,
1993).

The *Vishnudharmottara* is freely available online: Stella Kramrisch,
*The Vishnudharmottara Part III: A Treatise on Indian Painting
and Image-Making* (Calcutta: Calcutta University Press, 1928).

On pictorial organization in Japanese aesthetics, see Ken-ichi Sasaki,
Perspectives East and West. *Contemporary Aesthetics* 11 (2013):
spo.7523862.0011.016.

For more on surface and scene pictorial organization, see Bence
Nanay, Two-Dimensional versus Three-Dimensional Pictorial
Organization. *Journal of Aesthetics and Art Criticism* 73 (2015):
149–57.

The Baxandall quote is from his *Patterns of Intention* (New Haven:
Yale University Press, 1985), p. 109.

Further reading

Non-'Western' aesthetics

Heather Ahtone, Designed to Last: Striving towards an Indigenous American Aesthetics. *International Journal of the Arts in Society* 4 (2009): 373–85.

Zainab Bahrani, *The Graven Image: Representation in Babylonia and Assyria* (Philadelphia: University of Pennsylvania Press, 2003).

H. Gene Blocker, Non-Western Aesthetics as a Colonial Invention. *Journal of Aesthetic Education* 35 (2001): 3–13.

Stephen Davies, Balinese Aesthetics. *Journal of Aesthetics and Art Criticism* 65/1 (2007): 21–9.

Susan L. Feagin (ed.), *Global Theories of Art and Aesthetics*. Special issue of *Journal of Aesthetics and Art Criticism* 65/1 (2007).

Dominic Lopes, Shikinen Sengu and the Ontology of Architecture in Japan. *Journal of Aesthetics and Art Criticism* 65 (2007): 77–84.

Philip Rawson, The Methods of Zen Painting. *British Journal of Aesthetics* 7 (1967): 315–38.

Yuriko Saito, The Moral Dimension of Japanese Aesthetics. *Journal of Aesthetics and Art Criticism* 65/1 (2007): 85–97.

Susan P. Walton, Aesthetic and Spiritual Correlations in Javanese Gamelan Music. *Journal of Aesthetics and Art Criticism* 65/1 (2007): 31–41.

Robert Wicks, The Idealization of Contingency in Traditional Japanese Aesthetics. *Journal of Aesthetic Education* 39 (2005): 88–101.

Ajume H. Wingo, African Art and the Aesthetics of Hiding and Revealing. *British Journal of Aesthetics* 38 (1998): 251–64.

Aesthetics and art history/anthropology

Franz Boas, *Primitive Art* (Cambridge, Mass.: Harvard University Press, 1927).

Whitney Davis, *A General Theory of Visual Culture* (Princeton: Princeton University Press, 2011).

Roger Fry, *Vision and Design* (London: Chatto and Windus, 1920).

Clifford Geertz, *The Interpretation of Cultures* (New York: Basic Books, 1973).

Feminist and postcolonial aesthetics

Peg Brand (ed.), *Beauty Matters* (Bloomington, Ind.: Indiana University Press, 2000).

Peg Brand and Mary Devereaux (eds), *Women, Art, and Aesthetics*, Special issue of *Hypatia* 18/4 (2003).

Anne Eaton, Why Feminists Shouldn't Deny Disinterestedness. In: L. Ryan Musgrave (ed.), *Feminist Aesthetics and Philosophy of Art: The Power of Critical Visions and Creative Engagement* (New York: Springer, 2017).

Sherri Irvin, *Body Aesthetics* (Oxford: Oxford University Press, 2016).

Carolyn Korsmeyer, *Gender and Aesthetics* (London: Routledge, 2004).

Paul C. Taylor, *Black is Beautiful: A Philosophy of Black Aesthetics* (New York: Wiley, 2016).

Classic Anglo-American aesthetics

Monroe Beardsley, *Aesthetics*, 2nd edition (Indianapolis: Hackett, 1981).

Edward Bullough, 'Physical Distance' as a Factor in Art and as an Aesthetic Principle. *British Journal of Psychology* 5 (1912): 87–98.

John Dewey, *Art as Experience* (New York: Putnam, 1934).

Frank Sibley, Aesthetic and Nonaesthetic. *The Philosophical Review* 74/2 (1965): 135–59.

Jerome Stolnitz, *Aesthetics and Philosophy of Art Criticism* (New York: Houghton Mifflin, 1960).

Contemporary Anglo-American aesthetics

Malcolm Budd, *Values of Art* (London: Allen Lane, 1995).

Noël Carroll, *Beyond Aesthetics* (Cambridge: Cambridge University Press, 2001).

Diarmuid Costello, Kant and the Problem of Strong Non-perceptual Art. *British Journal of Aesthetics* 53 (2013): 277–98.

Robert Hopkins, *Picture, Image and Experience: A Philosophical Inquiry* (Cambridge: Cambridge University Press, 1998).

Matthew Kieran, *Revealing Art* (London: Routledge, 2005).

John Kulvicki, *On Images: Their Structure and Content* (Oxford: Oxford University Press, 2006).

Derek Matravers, Aesthetic Properties. *Proceedings of the Aristotelian Society* Supplementary Volume 79 (2005): 191–210.

Aaron Meskin, Mark Phelan, Margaret Moore, and Matthew Kieran, Mere Exposure to Bad Art. *British Journal of Aesthetics* 53 (2013): 139–64.

Elisabeth Schellekens, Towards a Reasonable Objectivism for Aesthetic Judgements. *British Journal of Aesthetics* 46/2 (2006): 163–77.

Kendall L. Walton, Categories of Art. *Philosophical Review* 79 (1970): 334–67.

Richard Wollheim, *Painting as an Art* (Princeton: Princeton University Press, 1987).

Nick Zangwill, *The Metaphysics of Beauty* (Ithaca, NY: Cornell University Press, 2001).

Index

Index

AFRICAN HISTORY
A Very Short Introduction
John Parker & Richard Rathbone

Essential reading for anyone interested in the African continent and the diversity of human history, this *Very Short Introduction* looks at Africa's past and reflects on the changing ways it has been imagined and represented. Key themes in current thinking about Africa's history are illustrated with a range of fascinating historical examples, drawn from over 5 millennia across this vast continent.

'A very well informed and sharply stated historiography...should be in every historiography student's kitbag. A tour de force...it made me think a great deal.'

Terence Ranger,
The Bulletin of the School of Oriental and African Studies

BEAUTY
A Very Short Introduction
Roger Scruton

In this *Very Short Introduction* the renowned philosopher Roger
Scruton explores the concept of beauty, asking what makes an
object - either in art, in nature, or the human form - beautiful,
and examining how we can compare differing judgements of
beauty when it is evident all around us that our tastes vary so
widely. Is there a right judgement to be made about beauty?
Is it right to say there is more beauty in a classical temple than
a concrete office block, more in a Rembrandt than in last year's
Turner Prize winner? Forthright and thought-provoking, and as
accessible as it is intellectually rigorous, this introduction to the
philosophy of beauty draws conclusions that some may find
controversial, but, as Scruton shows, help us to find greater
sense of meaning in the beautiful objects that fill our lives.

A fascinating book, which I heartily recommend.

Brya Wilson, Readers Digest

CRITICAL THEORY
A Very Short Introduction
Stephen Eric Bronner

In its essence, Critical Theory is Western Marxist thought with the emphasis moved from the liberation of the working class to broader issues of individual agency. Critical Theory emerged in the 1920s from the work of the Frankfurt School, the circle of German-Jewish academics who sought to diagnose--and, if at all possible, cure--the ills of society, particularly fascism and capitalism. In this book, Stephen Eric Bronner provides sketches of famous and less famous representatives of the critical tradition (such as George Lukács and Ernst Bloch, Theodor Adorno and Walter Benjamin, Herbert Marcuse and Jurgen Habermas) as well as many of its seminal texts and empirical investigations.

Early Music
A Very Short Introduction
Thomas Forrest Kelly

The music of the medieval, Renaissance, and baroque periods
have been repeatedly discarded and rediscovered ever since
they were new. In recent years interest in music of the past
has taken on particular meaning, representing two specific
trends: first, a rediscovery of little-known underappreciated
repertories, and second, an effort to recover lost performing
styles. In this VSI, Thomas Forrest Kelly frames chapters on
the forms, techniques, and repertories of the medieval,
Renaissance, and baroque periods with discussion of why old
music has been and should be revived, along with a short
history of early music revivals.

www.oup.com/vsi

FASHION
A Very Short Introduction
Rebecca Arnold

Fashion is a dynamic global industry that plays an important role in the economic, political, cultural, and social lives of an international audience. It spans high art and popular culture, and plays a significant role in material and visual culture. This book introduces fashion's myriad influences and manifestations. Fashion is explored as a creative force, a business, and a means of communication. From Karl Lagerfeld's creative reinventions of Chanel's iconic style to the multicultural reference points of Indian designer Manish Arora, from the spectacular fashion shows held in nineteenth century department stores to the mix-and-match styles of Japanese youth, the book examines the ways that fashion both reflects and shapes contemporary culture.

'Her fascinating little book makes a good framework for independent study and has a very useful bibliography.'

Philippa Stockley, Times Literary Supplement